Wm M Moore
JANUARY 1978

Buy, Sell, Merge:

How To Do It

BUY, SELL, MERGE:
HOW TO DO IT

WILLIAM H. BAUMER
and
LEO J. NORTHART

PRENTICE-HALL, INC.
Englewood Cliffs, N.J.

PRENTICE-HALL INTERNATIONAL, INC., *London*
PRENTICE-HALL OF AUSTRALIA, PTY. LTD., *Sydney*
PRENTICE-HALL OF CANADA, LTD., *Toronto*
PRENTICE-HALL OF INDIA PRIVATE LTD., *New Delhi*
PRENTICE-HALL OF JAPAN, INC., *Tokyo*

Library of Congress
Catalog Card Number: 70-164921

Printed in the United States of America

ISBN-O-13-109553-6
B & P

About the Authors

Photo by Fabian Bachrach

William H. Baumer is the President and member of the Board of Directors of International General Industries, Inc., Washington, D.C. In addition, Mr. Baumer holds Board membership in such firms as the Foster Wheeler Corporation, the Woodman Company, Kliklok Corporation, Globe Industries, Inc., and the Philadelphia Fund.

A member of the Council of Foreign Relations in New York, he has contributed to the Encyclopedia Brittanica, and has written numerous magazine articles. A graduate of Creighton University, the United States Military Academy, with an M.S. degree from Columbia, Mr. Baumer is also Major General in the U.S. Army Reserve. This is his ninth book.

Leo J. Northart is the Editorial Director and Business Manager for the Johnston International Publishing Corporation. He has 15 years' experience as a business writer, editor, lecturer and consultant on a wide variety of business subjects. The former editor of *Business Abroad,* Mr. Northart has also served as Managing Editor of *Dun's Review,* Editorial Director of Copley International Corporation and Manager of the International Management Division of the American Management Association.

A past President of the World Trade Writers of New York, he is the author of numerous articles and pamphlets on a wide range of business topics. Mr. Northart has been closely associated with top management in important aspects of merger technicalities as advisor, writer and speaker throughout the most dynamic period of merger activity in American history.

A WORD FROM THE AUTHORS

This book is written for the merger- and acquisition-minded executive and his financial and legal counsel. It departs from the usual approach to this subject and concentrates, instead, on the human factors involved. This book examines the motives, methods, and personal attitudes usually found behind the scenes of the purchase or sale of a company.

Toward this end we have presented 12 chapters, each dealing with a key phase in the often tricky, always exciting process of merging and acquiring. Each chapter is an attempt to take the reader deep into such situations as the delicate pre-merger negotiation, the decisive executive session, and the sensitive post-merger adjustment period.

Basically, this book is a "how-to-do-it" volume. It draws on personal experiences and focuses on the step-by-step approach to successful corporate "marriages," the pitfalls to be avoided, and the accepted but often over-looked protocol to be observed in such business transactions. Guidelines and rules of thumb are offered, as well as explanations of the facts and techniques behind the merger boom of the 1960s and the subsequent leveling off in the seventies. And there is a look ahead to a future of mergers and acquisitions without benefit of questionable financial sources and with some very interesting new rules.

Facts and figures, legal and tax complications, and price determinations have not been omitted. They are all here, but the emphasis is on the human factors. Through case histories, anecdotes and personal observations, you will be taken behind the facade of formal business discussions and to the very heart of merger and acquisition negotiations—the negotiating personalities themselves.

What this Book Will Do for You

This book is a how-to-do-it volume, but there is equal emphasis on "why." It will help you understand what motivates men to buy and sell companies and it will give you an insight into the human factors involved in mergers and acquisitions. Following are some of the questions that are raised and answered to provide you with guidelines for successful mergers:

- Why buy, sell, or merge? What brought about the merger boom of the 1960s? Why do men, particularly owners of privately, wholly owned companies, sell the results of their life's work? Is a merger a smart road to corporate growth? See Chapter 1.
- How do you conduct a successful search for an acquisition? What are the logical steps to take? How do company goals fit in? See Chapter 2.
- What can the "middleman" do for you? Who are they and what are their limitations? And what do you do about the sticky problem of fees? See Chapter 3.
- How do you handle the first meeting with the sellers? What can you expect to accomplish at this first get-together? Why is the whole process like a courtship between a boy and girl? See Chapter 4.
- What are the key questions to ask during the subsequent evaluation—financial, tax, growth potential, competition? And what about the human resources to be acquired—how do they fit in? See Chapter 5.
- Negotiating the deal is the trickiest phase. How do you do it? What goes on in the minds of buyer and seller? What is "tax-free reorganization" and how can it benefit you? What is "financial engineering" and why is it important to your deal? What kills the deal? See Chapter 6.
- How do tender offers and competing offers figure in? How can you defend against tender offers and against takeover? What is the "Performance Game" and how is it played? See Chapter 7.
- There are numerous governmental considerations. What are they and how do you cope with them? What are the agencies involved? Here is a seven-point checklist to guide you through this thorny phase of mergers and acquisitions. See Chapter 8.
- How do you reach a basic agreement, prepare a contract, and close the deal? What does the agreement contain—representations and warranties of buyer and seller, assets to be acquired, payment of purchase price, assumption of liabilities? What successful closing techniques should be observed? See Chapter 9.
- Post-merger adjustment is a difficult period. What are the key human factors to consider? What sort of control will work best? How can you be sure the "marriage" gets off to a good start? See Chapter 10.
- And what of the gigantic conglomerates? How did they get that way and what is their future? Who are the merger kings—the corporate giants who built the world's biggest corporations? What is the future of bank holding companies? See Chapter 11.
- How has the overseas merger movement affected U.S. corporations? How important are joint venture? How do they get started and where do they lead? See Chapter 12.

• How do you appraise a prospective purchase? What do you look for? Here is a 10-point checklist that will help you cover all the areas of information needed for a thorough investigation. See the Appendix.

William H. Baumer
Leo J. Northart

CONTENTS

Chapter 1

WHY COMPANIES BUY, SELL OR MERGE

The sale or merger of a company is generally the most important single decision a businessman will make in his corporate lifetime. The proper business decision in a matter of such magnitude requires penetrating analysis of corporate and self-interest. It also requires expert counsel in the major areas of consolidation planning; i.e. evaluation (of both buyer and seller), search, approach, negotiation, post-merger adjustment and consolidation. In fact, to bring about a successful merger, the first exploratory step should be initiated by a company's top management.

Today companies are merging at a rapid pace for a wide variety of reasons. But despite the popularity of corporate consolidations, thousands of companies will perform just as well without a new partner. Thousands of others, on the other hand, may benefit materially from a new association. Stock market conditions, of course, play a major part in such decisions; merger activity is up in a bull market, slower in a bear market.

Buying a Company

A company that has a successful acquisition program will obtain not only additional earnings, but, most likely, a higher price-earnings ratio for its stock. In effect, a good acquisition program feeds on itself. A company that is successful gets the most acquisition offerings—either directly from other companies that want to be associated with it or from intermediaries. Moreover, a rising price-earnings ratio gives a company a more valuable trading advantage in negotiations.

Acquisition is one way to make a company larger and potentially more profitable. Normally, a corporation intent on expansion will look either to new products developed from within, or to acquisition to achieve corporate objectives and to fulfill plans for growth. It is assumed, of course, that a company's management will consider the interplay of all factors—finance, marketing, personnel, and production—in their business strategy, and that they will carefully analyze their objectives and what they hope to accomplish before making an acquisition decision. To achieve basic objectives of making the company larger, more successful and more profitable, there are many alternatives that should be looked into. A steadily increasing number of companies are turning to acquisition to attain these objectives.

Factors Which Motivate Acquisition

Both public and private companies enter into the world of acquisition. However, since most privately owned companies are small and do not have the capital or stock to acquire other companies, they usually do not think of purchasing other corporate entities. Occasionally, though, there will be a merger of two privately owned companies, but the sum of these activities is not large. Most acquisitions involve publicly held companies in the manufacturing, finance, mining, or service industries.

Expansion and growth are not the only valid reasons for acquiring another firm. There are dozens of reasons for making acquisitions beyond the desire to add new products or plants. Many business objectives can be fulfilled by acquiring other companies, such as strengthening the company's financial position, obtaining the services of key personnel, obtaining technical skills, and achieving integration. There are even companies that seek to acquire others merely to give the appearance of being a dynamic corporation with aggressive people at its head.

But despite the popularity of mergers and acquisitions, there are some large corporations in America that have not acquired other companies for many years. Sometimes such reluctance has been short sighted because management has denied to its organization the potential benefits in an acquisition. Sometimes the executives of these companies have been fearful of the consequences of an acquisition since, invariably, they would be sticking their necks out by claiming that it would add to the profitability and success of their own corporations.

Setting Realistic Goals

Acquisition of itself does not automatically solve the problems of a corporation, nor is success assured. In fact, when an acquisition is considered, it should be remembered that along with the acquisition come many problems which are alien to the day-to-day operations of a business. Only by acquisition, however, can corporate management learn what these problems are.

The first step in any acquisition program is to examine requirements and determine objectives. These should be set in terms of products, special strengths, size, and return on investment. Priorities should be established so that the most important acquisition areas are explored first and other companies of lower priority are left to later consideration. Priorities will change, of course, as the result of acquisitions or growth of the business and should be reevaluated and realigned as frequently as necessary.

One way to establish priorities is to determine which strengths your company most needs, such as management, distribution, product line, technology, production, cash, or some form of vertical or horizontal integration. Some companies set per-share earnings contribution as their goal.

There are many reasons for acquiring companies. We have listed and will discuss some 13 of them, including growth, investment, diversification, new products, patents, personnel, market distribution, uneven business cycles, time, technical know-how, integration (to obviate a possible loss of market), new developments, and tax loss carry-forwards.

Projecting Growth Dynamics

When executives gather at business conferences, they invariably speak of their companies' successes with such statements as, "We had sales last year of $70 million and this year we expect to do $100 million." You can imagine what effect this has on the president of a small corporation that is perhaps enjoying a profitable $10 or $20 million sales volume. When he returns home, he naturally thinks of ways that he can expand his company so that he can belong to the fraternity of presidents of larger companies. He logically thinks of how he might acquire companies that would help him expand and grow in a successful way. Or, conversely, he may think of selling his company—particularly if he or his associates own large blocks of his company's stock.

Besides size and profits there are many other reasons for desiring growth, such as expansion into new territories and the addition of new product lines. These will be considered later under their respective headings.

Dovetailing the Acquisition

In contemplating growth through acquisition, the management and board of directors of the corporation must think in terms of expansion of sales volume and, hopefully, of profits. For example, executives of a company in the automotive parts field may feel that since it is supplying custom-built axles, it could expand into a similar type of metal product such as engine parts or transmissions. The key word is compatibility since it is necessary that a company look to its immediate environment. A company like Babcock & Wilcox, which has been building power plants for generations, has looked for acquisitions in fields such as firebrick, boilers, generators, steel tubes, and even in the valve and other equipment fields. All of these business areas are relevant to its major purpose and its acquisitions have fulfilled a need and have been responsible for growth in both sales and earnings.

Measuring Investment Potential

The reason usually given for an acquisition is that it is "a good investment." This would be a good reason, for example, for a company whose earnings were $2 a share and whose stock was selling at a multiple of, say, 20 times that, or $40 a share, if the board of directors were looking around for a smaller company that would add 50 cents to corporate earnings. Naturally, the financial men would be brought in to determine how much would have to be paid for the company. But, if the company could be bought for a convertible preferred stock with a 7 to 8 percent dividend rate, the cost to the acquiring company hopefully would be more than offset by the earnings which would be brought in by the acquisition.

It should also be noted that in some cases fast-growing, diversified, and conglomerate companies short of cash have grabbed for an acquisition, particularly a private company, with a large bundle of cash among its assets. Once the company is acquired, the extra cash or cash assets can be converted to the uses of the owning company.

In looking at a potential acquisition, however, the corporation may find that it is courting an old company whose assets have been heavily depreciated, but one that can be recapitalized at a higher figure if assets are purchased. All three approaches add to the financial strength of the acquiring company and are considered "good business" in the merger and acquisition world.

Key Reasons for Diversification

The reasons behind diversification moves are usually rather apparent. In many defense industry concentrations, for example, there is an expressed desire to decrease the percentage of business done with the federal government and increase the share done in the commercial field. Quite often, one will read of a defense-oriented company that does as much as 80 percent of its business with the government. In such cases, there usually is a demand by the board of directors and by management for the acquisition of compatible, non-defense companies in which the defense industry capabilities may be used. There is, however, a danger in this course of action since defense industry specifications and requirements usually require a company to maintain standards of performance beyond those required in normal commercial practice. There have been cases where defense-oriented firms were unable to compete economically in other fields. The alternative is to purchase a non-defense-related company that is almost autonomous in its own field and operate it as a subsidiary.

Cases in Point: The Pharmaceutical Industry

A good example of diversification is the drug company that looks beyond the prescription fields of pills and potions to compatible areas such as proprietary drugs, over-the-counter products, food and household products, cosmetics, hospital supplies, medical electronics, chemical companies, agricultural chemicals, and laboratories. There is no question that the drug companies have looked at the mounting costs of research for wonder drugs, and have become concerned about the federal regulatory agencies and the restrictive requirements placed upon new products before they can be released for public consumption.

Exploding a Myth

One pharmaceutical executive has stated that the myth should be dispelled that the industry's ills are caused solely by politicians. He said that the facade of "government intervention" conceals more than it explains. The slow-down in new product productivity has come at the very time when many companies are facing profit erosion from the expiration of patents on old products. Where previously drug companies achieved growth by relying on good research, now they are building defensive platoons in the form of diversified interests in allied areas.

The Case of Merck & Company

Mr. Henry W. Gadsden, president of Merck & Company, Inc., has taken cognizance of his industry's new activity by saying that it is no coincidence that since the attacks on the drug industry have continued, every one of the major drug firms has moved toward diversification. All of them have developed new business in other fields including those mentioned before, as well as Merck's acquisition of the Calgon Corporation.

There is no suggestion that the ethical drug manufacturers are abandoning their laboratories since Merck alone budgeted some $69 million in research and development work in the 1970s. Many of the smaller and medium-sized drug firms are also increasing their research and development expenditures.

The diversification activities of the ethical drug companies have been widespread. Abbott Laboratories, for example, has acquired a hospital supply company, and Merck has moved into the chemical field. A.H. Robbins has acquired companies producing proprietary drug, food and household products, cosmetics, and agriculture and animal health products. J.D. Searle has acquired a company in the medical electronics field, as well as a major laboratory. Syntex has diversified into the chemical area and Upjohn has acquired an electronics firm and has also entered into the chemical field.

There is usually a basic reason for diversifying. In the cases mentioned, it was a need to decrease dependency upon defense industry business, or, in part, as in the case of the drug industry, to get away from "too much" government regulation. There are also examples of diversification purely for investment and growth as seen in the acquisitions of Walter Kidde & Company, Continental Can, and many other large corporations.

Expansion Through New Products

Many companies, both large and small, purchase other companies in order to add new products to their lines. Owens-Illinois Inc., the nation's leading manufacturer of glass containers, acquired the Lily-Tulip Cup Corporation through an exchange of shares valued at more than $141 million. Owens-Illinois manufactures glass containers (including electronic and scientific glassware), glass tableware, container board, corrugated shipping containers, and blown plastic bottles. Lily-Tulip manufactures disposable paper and plastic containers, plates and dishes, and table utensils, along with food packages such as ice cream containers.

Other examples of mergers in which the addition of new products was a major objective include Signal Companies' acquisition of Mack Trucks; Studebaker's acquisition of Worthington, which specializes in industrial pumps (creating Studebaker-Worthington); and SCM Corporation's acquisition of Glidden and a paint line that gave SCM a whole new area of interest. When Ling-Tempco-Vought acquired Wilson Packing Corporation in one of the big conglomerate deals of 1967, it acquired not only a line of packing-house products but also a sporting goods company, which was spun off in 1970 to PepsiCo. American Can acquired the Marathon Paper Company and got a foothold in the paperboard industry. That acquisition, in 1957, was one of the largest of the period, involving the acquisition of assets valued at $168.9 million. In 1970, Coca-Cola made its first major diversification move outside of the food and beverage field with its acquisition of Aqua-Chem (Milwaukee, Wis.), a manufacturer of water pollution control equipment. Coca-Cola issued 1,754,000 common shares valued at $130 million on the basis of one share for each 1.3115 shares of Aqua-Chem. The acquired company, which also makes equipment for desalting sea and brackish water and a line of steam generating systems, is operating as a Coca-Cola subsidiary.

In one of the large deals of 1970, Greyhound acquired Armour and Company after a period of controversy that lasted well over a year. The deal was approved prior to consummation by the ICC, but the Justice Department then filed suit to dissolve the merger. However, a request by the Antitrust Division that Greyhound be enjoined from controlling Armour was denied by a Federal District Judge. He rejected the Justice Department's claim that the acquisition violated a 1920 consent decree prohibiting meat packing companies from expanding into certain food lines and other products.

This step in the battle for control of Armour (assets $607,224,000) was finalized with Greyhound's official closing of its acquisition from General Host Corporation of a controlling interest in Armour. Greyhound, in a 1969 tender offer, acquired 33 percent of Armour common stock, and the acquisition of the General Host interest gave Greyhound 86 percent control of Armour. For General Host's stock interest, Greyhound offered a package of cash, notes, preferred stock and warrants to buy Greyhound common stock. Specifically, the agreement called for the following: $77 million in cash and "an amount representing an adjustment for interest on debentures and dividends on the common stock"; a 5-year $36.5 million promissory note of Greyhound bearing interest at the prime rate of the principal commercial banks of New York City on the day prior to the date of issue; 800,000 shares of $5 convertible preference stock of Greyhound having a stated value of $100 per share, each share convertible into five shares of Greyhound common stock; 10-year common stock purchase warrants to buy 4.25 million shares of Greyhound common at a price of $23.50 or $24 per share, depending on the stock price immediately prior to the date the transaction is consummated.

How Patents Fit into the Picture

In times past it was rather common for a company to acquire another because the latter held certain patents that allowed for development of new lines of products. However, as patent protection appears to be more difficult to maintain, particularly abroad, there is less interest than previously in acquiring a company solely for patent rights. One reason for this is that today many process patents can be circumvented by the development of similar methods of production, which can open up new areas for a company without the necessity of acquiring another simply for its patents. Bear in mind, however, that there is a distinction between patents and know-how. Acquisition of know-how—technical, marketing or managerial—may very well be a valid reason for buying a company *(see below)*. It is important that in all acquisitions the parties check for patents, basic patents as well as design patents, since these have an asset value for both the selling and the acquiring companies.

Buying Managerial Expertise

There have been a number of occasions when an acquisition was billed as being for the purpose of obtaining certain management talent, usually a president or some highly technical specialists whom the acquiring company wanted. However, this alone is a risky reason since something might happen to the individual or he might not work out well in his new spot, particularly if the acquiring company is thinking of utilizing his talents as its president. However, there have been a number of mergers in which a larger company acquired a somewhat smaller one with the objective of utilizing the president of the smaller company as the new president of the overall company. Most certainly, if the acquisition of management talent is an important consideration, it is important to determine that the company has management depth. Otherwise, the loss of a few key people could nullify a major reason for the purchase.

Much more common is the purchase of smaller companies for market distribution and sales forces. In a way, this also is buying time since the creation and establishment of a national sales force for a product line can take a long time—often several years—and is usually fraught with many difficulties. Many acquisitions have been spawned when a company has wanted to expand its sales territory and geographical coverage by purchasing a smaller company doing an excellent job in the desired sales territory. This method of acquisition works best when the acquired product line is very similar, even competitive.

Understanding Business Cycles

A number of acquisitions over the past ten years have been consummated for the purpose of helping to even out the business cycles in the industry in which the acquiring company is operating. This has been true particularly in heavy industry and in building products, where there are cycles of five, seven, nine or more years. There are many engineering and large heavy-industry companies whose business cycles are such that they are almost certain, at some period in the coming few years, to run out of orders and experience a decline in both sales and profits. Usually the percentage decline in profits is greater than that in sales, primarily because the cutback in personnel usually lags behind the drop in sales. In the expectation that business will turn up, employees with certain skills must be retained.

The optimum time for such a company to make an acquisition is when it is at the high point or near the high point of its cycle in both sales volume and profits. Unfortunately, because of it cyclical business, the company is unable to use its market position to get a favorable stock market value on its common shares or preferred stock in an acquisition move. Most likely, any attractive company in similar or compatible kinds of industrial categories will have a profit margin that is more inclined to be stable, or to be rising, and not subject to the sharp rise and fall common to cyclical industries.

Buying Time

Making an acquisition to buy time is particularly common among newly organized companies and, to a lesser degree, among conglomerates. The objective of these companies is to grow as rapidly as possible in sales volume and earnings, and to expand into new lines of endeavor. It would seem obvious that one quick way to get a favorable position in a new line would be to buy a company already in that field and to use it as a base upon which to expand. For example, when Litton Industries was a new company some 15 years ago, its top management worked out a plan for growth internally and through acquisition. After entering the microwave and electronics fields, the company made plans for getting into the office equipment business. Their alternatives were to develop from within or to create an entry into the market by purchasing another company. After evaluation, it was obvious to management that creation of a national sales and service organization for office equipment would be costly and time consuming and that it would be far easier to acquire a company already established in the field. After considering a number of possibilities, negotiations were initiated with the Monroe Calculating Machine Company, which at that time had 350 company-owned sales and service branches in the United States. Monroe was acquired in late 1957, establishing a market for Litton in the office equipment field.

In a related vein, a company of substantial size will from time to time develop a new product as a result of research that it may not have the essential manufacturing and marketing organization to handle. Many of America's largest corporations have had this experience. Research in chemicals, drugs, and many other fields have created products that were outside the companies' normal product lines. The decision then is whether to sell the product to someone in that line or to purchase a company that would have both the manufacturing and sales capabilities required. There is no one "best" answer; it depends on a host of variables that pertain at the time. Suffice it to say that such a situation does create a climate for acquisition.

Building Technical Know-How

During the technological revolution of the past 20 years, acquisitions often have been based on the fact that the companies being purchased had technical know-how that would be of great value to the purchasers. One reason for this is that there are today a large number of technical firms with "think tanks," which are primarily groups of Ph.D.s in science who have a capability much needed by the more prosaic operating manufacturing companies. Many acquisitions have brought about the union of these two dissimilar corporate entities. Usually the technical company is small and many of the acquisitions go relatively unnoticed except in scientific circles. In Boston, Washington, and Palo Alto, California, for example, there are large numbers of science-oriented companies that do not produce goods or products but which concentrate on the development of specific scientific know-how. These companies are often established with the expectation that after they have made themselves known, they will be purchased by larger companies better able to utilize the scientific experience and knowledge in the production and marketing of products.

Vertical Integration

Basically, vertical acquisition to achieve integration means simply that the acquiring company is seeking a source of supply which may extend back from straight manufacturing as far as the forest or the mine. In recent years, there has been a return to, or at least a greater emphasis on, achieving control of the source of supply and of ancillary equipment.

In the nuclear field, for example, there must be mining of various nuclear elements, processing, and eventually their use in power plants. In June 1968, Combustion Engineering, Incorporated, took a position in the nuclear extraction field by purchasing 21 percent of United Nuclear Corporation. A U.S. District Court declared in 1969 that this purchase was a violation of the Clayton Act. A decision was reached in November 1969, whereby Combustion would be required to dispose of its United Nuclear holdings within ten years. In addition, many of the companies in the business of building nuclear power plants are also acquiring other nuclear companies specializing in valves, instruments, pumps, and other components needed for the power plant.

In the past, companies in the paper producing industry have sought to bring about integration by securing ownership of everything from forests to processing plants to manufacturing plants turning out the final product. Kimberly-Clark is a good example of this kind of integration.

Oil companies, too, have increasingly sought integration by purchasing petroleum companies specializing in marketing or extraction.

Anticipating Possible Loss of Market

This area has received a great deal of interest recently, particularly in the tobacco field. Stimulated by the government's campaign to warn users of the possible dangers of smoking cigarettes, there has been an increasing tendency for cigarette makers to diversify to meet expected changes in consumer habits and, if possible, to compensate for any decrease in the sales of their basic products.

One observer has noted that the tobacco companies seem to be operating under the theory that if we stop smoking we will do a lot more eating. The U.S. tobacco companies at first glance seem to be diversifying primarily into food and drink. For example, American Tobacco, now American Brands, has bought Duffy-Mott Company, a New York-based food processor. Until 1967, tobacco accounted for 100 percent of American's sales, but by the end of 1970 the figure had been cut to 77 percent through acquisition of Sunshine Biscuits, Inc., and James B. Beam Distilling Company.

Liggett & Myers

In addition, all the other tobacco companies have exhibited similar acquisition tastes. Liggett & Myers, which was already in the imported liquors and wines business, cereal products, and pet foods, bought Austin, Nichols & Company—a liquor distributor and importer. The range of activities acquired by the tobacco companies is indicated by Philip Morris in chewing gum; British-American in ice cream; R.J. Reynolds Tobacco Company in foods; and Lorillard Corporation, part of Loews Corp. in candy.

Other Examples in the Tobacco Industry

Some of the tobacco companies have ranged even farther afield in their acquisitions. Philip Morris, which is now about 20 percent non-tobacco, is in razors and blades, paper, packaging, textile chemicals, beer, hospital products, and toiletries. Recently Philip Morris agreed to acquire the remaining 47 percent of the outstanding shares of the Miller Brewing Company, having acquired 53 percent of the Miller shares from W.R. Grace in 1969 in a transaction valued at $130 million. British-American, now 14 percent non-tobacco, is in packaging, printing, perfumes, and cosmetics. R.J. Reynolds, 35 percent non-tobacco, is in aluminum, transportation, packaging, and industrial corn products. Lorillard, now part of Loews Corporation and only 5 percent non-tobacco, is in candy.

The presidents of the tobacco companies have stated that the industrial trend is only one of concern over possible future decreases in tobacco sales; all stress that the tobacco business is very much alive. But despite their denials, many of the companies are seeking up to 40 percent or 50 percent of their sales in areas outside of tobacco.

New Developments: Getting in on the Ground Floor

In years past, the new developments were concentrated heavily in the electronics and nuclear fields, but today the wave of the future seems to be breaking over such varied areas as oceanography, lasers, and irradiation of food and other products. Many a large company feeling that it can afford to purchase a small but growing company in one of these fields, and accepting at first either small losses or a breakeven situation, will buy a company that is beginning to make its mark in one of these glamour industries. Such decisions are the result of evaluation and long-range planning by larger companies and are indicative of an ability to be flexible and to find new areas which five to ten years from now may mean profits for the company.

Many of the drug firms, and occasionally other similarly sized firms, will advertise that a large percentage, perhaps as much as 25 percent to 50 percent, of their products were unknown 10 or 15 years ago. It is this pioneering drive coupled with sound business acumen that creates acquisition-minded companies and causes them to seek new areas to enter.

Tax Loss Carry-Forward

The acquisition-minded company will from time to time run into a smaller company with a rather sizable tax loss carry-forward. This is a tax advantage that must be approached with caution. A review of the pertinent federal laws indicates that in the acquisition of a company with a tax loss carry-forward (tax shelter), it is essential to continue in the same business and to retain the operation in the same location for at least two years, preferably until such time as the tax loss is utilized. A company purchasing another with a tax shelter must ask itself a number of very important questions. Most important is whether the company can get out of its loss position and contribute to the profit side of the ledger. Another question is whether the business is within the range of experience of the management of the acquiring firm and whether it is one which they have solid reason to believe they can turn around.

Tax losses as a factor in acquisitions can be worth from nothing to as much as 50 percent of the total amount. Those companies with tax shelters are of value to a company if it believes that it can make a profit in that line and if there is some compatibility in the product lines. Also, tax shelters are usually found in smaller companies and sometimes the amount is rather staggering compared to the net worth or the negative net worth of the company.

It is highly doubtful whether an acquiring company should ever buy another company merely because it has a tax loss. It does occur, however, that some companies losing money still have highly qualified engineers and scientists but lack marketing know-how and the organizational skill to properly automate the plant. There are a number of cases in which the company with the tax loss was a job-shop operation that had grown too big for its own britches and was unable to make the giant step into an assembly line operation. Occasionally, therefore, an acquiring company can readily supply needed know-how and, with good fortune and a great deal of work, make the company profitable, thereby utilizing the tax loss.

Factors Motivating the Seller

Again and again the question is asked of selling companies: "Why do you wish to sell?" Quite often a company that is well managed and profitable will be purchased, to everyone's surprise, by another company. Was the sale made for personal, business, product, or financial reasons, or was there another motivation for the sale?

There are usually two major types of sales of companies: the first is the disposition of divisions and subsidiaries by large companies; and the second is the sale of either a small or large public company or, often, a privately owned company.

In the first type, the sell-off of divisions and subsidiaries, there has been increasing activity in recent years. One observer listed the following five forces that compel the selling of certain corporate entities:

1. Because of an antitrust decision, a company is compelled to sell a sizable chunk of its holdings. The Maremont Corporation received such a notice in July 1968 demanding that it sell 40 units or companies that had been acquired since 1953. A spokesman for the company said that if such a sell-off was accomplished it would reduce the earnings volume of the company by more than half.

2. Corporate management has become more sensitive to divisional profit reporting and the losers are detected and sold off quicker than in former years. There is a status loss for the management that keeps a loser going and a gain in status for the company that sells such a loser.

3. The Securities and Exchange Commission has issued statutory regulations to compel corporations to publish divisional earnings reports. This regulation will undoubtedly cause a rush to sell off losers before the investment community and the stockholders learn the facts.

4. Even without SEC regulations, there is a fourth reason for selling off divisions. With the growing focus on conglomerates, there is certain to be more criticism of managements which hang on to losers. Part of this problem is the question of "corporate image," which is important to companies today and, therefore, a good reason for re-examining all those divisions that fail to live up to profit expectations.

5. A sell-off is one way to get capital quickly and, thereby, to look good in the earnings column.

Examples of Successful Sell-Offs

Examples of corporate sell-offs include that of the American Can Company, which had operating losses for several years in its glass container business. It sold its glass facilities and inventories to Midland Glass Company, Inc. in a deal expected to generate a cash flow of approximately $25 million and to represent a nonrecurring loss of about $16 million after taxes that would be reflected against 1967 net income. There is also the example of the SCM Corporation which sold its Data Processing Systems Division for an undisclosed amount of cash to Control Data Corporation.

Studebaker-Worthington Corporation sold its Franklin Appliance Division to White Consolidated Industries for something under the book value of approximately $21 million, explaining that the division was in a field not compatible with the present and future intended areas of corporate investment. White Consolidated Industries also acquired an "unprofitable operation" in the Davidson Division of Fairchild Camera & Instrument Corporation. Davidson, which makes offset process equipment, office meter machines and similar items, had been a drag on Fairchild profits.

General Dynamics Corporation sold its General Atomic Division to the Gulf Oil Corporation. General Atomic, located in La Jolla, California, employed over 2,000 workers and, as a technological company, engaged in research, produced nuclear fuel, and furnished nuclear systems for electric power plants.

Basic Reasons Why Companies are Sold

1. Limited Product Line

Small companies in the electronics, nuclear, oil, data processing, and other fast-moving fields may find that because of the lack of capital, or lack of technical know-how or research, they have too limited a product line. The sales force cannot approach a customer and meet his full line of needs. In a rapidly changing field, a limited product line can be disastrous. Thus, some companies, after evaluating their prospects, feel that it would be better to sell the company to beef up the line of a larger company rather than to attempt to go it alone in their own expansion program.

2. Increasing Competition

The managements of smaller public and private companies are painfully aware of the fact that the number of competing companies continues to grow. In some fields it is quite noticeable that there will be only three, four, or five companies producing a certain specific product for the same market. As time goes on, others enter the field and new companies or divisions and subsidiaries of larger companies are created. When eight or nine companies are bidding for a relatively slow-growing market, there is not room for all and sales are bound to suffer. When this happens, the smaller company will begin to seek a chance to merge with a larger one, or to sell out altogether.

3. Shrinking Profit Margins

Many smaller companies exist in a highly competitive situation in an industrial area and find that after a number of years of reasonably good profit margins, a shrinkage begins to occur. Then the managements or the owners determine that perhaps they had better sell before the margins sink so low that their companies will not be worth much to a prospective purchaser.

4. Market Saturation

In many fields of industrial manufacturing, there is relative market saturation by existing products. This is particularly true for industrial markets, for which new products have been created at a slower rate than for other areas. For example, market saturation appeared fairly often in the machine tool industry where, in certain periods, there was an overcapacity and a shrinking profit margin for existing products. However, the development of numerical controls made obsolete most of the old-line machine tools and created a new market. Here is an example of a prior market saturation being eliminated by the development of a wholly new line of products.

In a somewhat similar field, textile machinery, a significant number of companies gradually disappeared because of market saturation, which resulted in part from the long life of the machines that were developed. This forced some companies out of business and caused others to turn to different product lines.

5. Expiring Patents

The rather comfortable 17-year life of patents has enabled many companies to grow strong and flex their muscles because they have had protection against copying and other forms of infringement.

A company that has lived for a long period on one or more patents, however, faces a real crisis when the patent nears the expiration date. There are examples where patent-oriented managements have failed to push into new lines through acquisition, merger, or development of new products, with the result that when patent expiration was two or three years away, they were faced with having to sell their companies. They found that shortly they would have nothing of an exclusive nature to market.

6. Inadequate Financing

Probably, inadequate financing plagues small private and public companies more than any other factor of business. This is not to say that large industrial corporations do not suffer from this problem as well, but usually they are able to find some source of financing or to make other moves that resolve the problem. Small companies can suffer from inadequate financing both if business is bad and if business is growing rapidly. There is nothing unusual about this. It is a question of cash flow. A company that has been a steady loser has to find new financing and if all avenues are blocked, the only alternative is to sell.

On the other hand, quite often a company through wise management and the development of new products and new markets grows at an unbelievably fast rate. The demands for new plant, new equipment, or handling of receivables and inventory, grow so rapidly that it is impossible to find the necessary financing from the usual banking and investment areas. In this case, management will often turn to the possibility of a sale, although here the situation is more pleasant because usually the company has a good asset value and is a desirable catch for an acquisition-minded firm.

Another consideration is a company's bank balance. Is it so fat that it invites a takeover? If the balance sheet reveals an unusually large amount of quick assets in relation to total assets, which varies by industry, this could attract a takeover bid.

7. Thinness of Management

From time to time, the reason given for the sale of a company is that the management was inadequate for the company's development. This sounds as if there was complete failure to search for the proper personnel. There have been many instances when a single owner has kept the reins solidly in his own hands and has been slow to develop executives, or was of such character that it was impossible for others to develop under him. Therefore, the normal second and third lines of management have left the company rather than face the frustration of dealing with the single owner. In such cases, when the owner-manager faces retirement, or dies, the company must be sold.

Since many companies are privately owned, or are smaller public companies with large blocks of stocks owned by a relatively small number of people, the desire of the principals to retire brings about an immediate demand to sell because their wealth is tied up in the one business asset. Estate problems and taxes are a constant concern to small companies, particularly where two or three men own the company and have a substantial part of their worldly goods tied up in it.

In one case, two owners, not of advanced age at all, decided to sell their company because they were concerned that one of them might lose his life as a result of the substantial amount of air travel required. The death of one or both would have caused tremendous challenges and problems for the estates and for the business itself. Often, the wives of partners or of the owners of public and private companies have a great influence on their husbands. The general line of discussion is that the husbands have worked hard and long and have achieved some very desirable results, but everything is tied up in the company. The wives may argue, "You have worked hard now for 30 years, let's travel and enjoy the fruits of your labors." In many such cases, the individuals gradually get the point and decide to sell.

In two known cases, owners of companies have had their wish to sell intensified by the fact that none of their progeny had any interest in the business. The new generation, perhaps better educated than their fathers and more affluent because of their fathers' work, felt that their interests were more diversified, leaning, perhaps, to the professions or science rather than the making of widgets.

Emotions as a Factor in the Sale

One writer in the field of mergers and acquisitions maintains that fear is the underlying motivation for the sale of many companies. He explored the idea of fear of financial needs, of competition, of a host of other problems which are the daily challenges of any business. This idea is not readily accepted because discussions with large numbers of potential sellers have revealed that if there is fear, and there is always some, usually it is well covered by an expression of a desire to move into other lines, or to retire, or to be rid of the cares of business.

Finally, it should be noted in passing that, fortunately, the sale of a business oftentimes does not mean the loss of position or job. Many acquiring companies are anxious that the management remain in the active operation of the business. If the former owner-managers are anxious to leave, they usually are retained as consultants. Such men with long experience in the company have acquaintances and knowledge of the industry that can be of use to the acquiring company.

Thus, there are many reasons for sale or merger, including poor return on invested capital, the need for expanded production facilities, the need for greater market distribution, the need for larger expenditures for research and development in order to bring the product line up to date, and a host of personal preferences. These and many other impelling reasons motivate a controlling shareholder or owners to explore the possibility of merger.

Games Managers Play

Before proceeding to a discussion, in subsequent chapters, of the fundamentals of buying, selling, and merging, it is worth noting that this complex management "game" is not without its lighter side. David Dempsey, writing on publishing mergers in the July 13, 1968 issue of *Saturday Review* strikes a humorous note.

"There used to be a saying," Dempsey writes, "about mergers in publishing that as the companies got bigger they got smaller." It wasn't always true, but it happened often enough so that two ailing publishers, joined together, might do less business than before—Darwinism in reverse, or the survival of the unfit.

"Today publishers get bigger when they merge, but the significant change is in the variety of ways in which this happens. Between 1962 and 1967, 124 publishers underwent some kind of corporate change of life—merger, sellout, takeover, stock purchase, or what have you. In the merger-happy climate of the modern business world, this is all part of the game. The question is, what game?"

Mr. Dempsey goes on to list ten ways of interpreting the next announcement you read concerning a publishing merger. His interpretations, based on information from the recently published *Bowker Book Annual of Library and Book Trade Information, 1968* (R. R. Bowker & Company), include the following:

THE NUMBERS GAME. Object is to acquire as many smaller firms as possible in order to make a big company bigger. In the 1962-67 trial heat McGraw-Hill led with seven deals. The Times-Mirror Company of Los Angeles was second with five. But Times-Mirror had a handicap of two, since it was not in the book publishing business to start with.

FULL CIRCLE, or the Oedipal game. This is the trickiest one of all. Back in the forties, Pocket Books was started by Simon & Schuster. Then Field Enterprises bought both companies. Some years ago, Pocket Books bought itself back from Field, and in 1966 acquired the original parent company, Simon & Schuster. All contestants return to Go.

THE LEVERAGE GAME. When a bought-out publisher (Silver Burdette) is used as an investment (by Time, Inc.) in a new joint enterprise (with General Electric) the result is General Learning.

Mr. Dempsey goes on to say, "Has all this made publishing any different? Not much. Books are still written by men and women sitting at typewriters in lonely rooms, and that the typewriters might be IBM models hasn't made it any easier. Editors still louse up manuscripts (or improve them) . . . The merger game has reached its climacteric, and at this point no one can decide whether to send for the doctor or a certified public accountant."

Chapter 2

CONDUCTING THE SEARCH

Before any company seriously considers an acquisition, merger, or sale, it should make a thorough evaluation of its goals and prospects. In most large companies this study is part of long-range planning, but in many smaller companies, a long-range plan may be only partially written or may exist only in the mind of the owner-manager. The charting of a company's future growth must take into consideration the two alternatives of growth from within and expansion from without. In most successful companies both areas are subject to a great deal of study, and in most companies both avenues are explored and developed to the full.

The normal method of handling the corporation's future planning for acquisitions is to divide the function into its three significant parts: establishing objectives; defining criteria to meet those objectives; and organizing to fulfill the objectives.

How Successful Companies Execute the Plan

Some companies such as Indianhead Metals, state that their explicit objective is to increase the value of the common stock. On the other hand, Charles W. Percy, when president of Bell & Howell, stated the company's goals this way: "We believe firmly that our business should be the expression of the ideas and objectives of our entire management group and, as far as humanly possible, of our employee group."

General Robert Wood Johnson, the late chairman of the Johnson & Johnson Company, expressed the goal of business progress in an industrial credo that is statesmanlike, yet realistic and down-to-earth, as follows:

> We believe that our first responsibility is to the doctors, nurses, hospitals, mothers, and all others who use our products. Our products must always be of the highest quality. We must constantly strive to reduce the cost of these products. Our orders must be promptly and accurately filled. Our dealers must make a fair profit.

> Our second responsibility is to those who work with us—the men and women in our plants and offices. They must have a sense of security in their jobs. Wages must be fair and adequate, management just, hours reasonable, and working conditions clean and orderly. Employees should have an organized system for suggestions and complaints. Supervisors and department heads must be qualified and fair-minded. There must be opportunity for advancement—for those qualified—and each person must be considered an individual standing on his own dignity and merit.
>
> Our third responsibility is to our management. Our executives must be persons of talent, education, experience and ability. They must be persons of common sense and full understanding.
>
> Our fourth responsibility is to the communities in which we live. We must be a good citizen—support good works and charity, and bear our fair share of taxes. We must maintain in good order the property we are privileged to use. We must participate in promotion of civic improvement, health, education and good government, and acquaint the community with our activities.
>
> Our fifth and last responsibility is to our stockholders. Business must make a sound profit. Reserves must be created, research must be carried on, adventurous programs developed, and mistakes paid for. Adverse times must be provided for, adequate taxes paid, new machines purchased, new plants built, new products launched, and new sales plans developed. We must experiment with new ideas. When these things have been done the stockholder should receive a fair return. We are determined with the help of God's grace to fulfill these obligations to the best of our ability.

It is interesting to note that General Johnson's statement made no specific reference to acquisitions, and that for many years Johnson & Johnson did not widen or expand its interests other than by the development of new products. In recent years, the company has purchased a number of companies and expanded its operations into other areas. However, such acquisitions were within the scope of this finely worded credo.

Within the Johnson credo there are expressed a number of basic corporate objectives relating to finance, marketing, manufacturing, personnel, research and development, and community relations. It strongly emphasized equitable working conditions and the dignity of labor. It also recognizes the company's responsibility for developing management and its responsibility to owners and stockholders.

Establishing Financial Goals

A basic consideration in all corporate planning is profitability, or adequate return on investment. Of course, this would vary according to the size of the company, type of industry and, probably, according to the age of the company. Return on investment is very meaningful to operating management, to the board of directors, to the investment community, and to stockholders. In fact, a basic question for merger-minded executives is: What will the per-share earnings of the original stockholders be in the enlarged corporation after a reasonable period of time?

The financial community has a term, *acquisition synergism,* used to explain the unique benefit arising out of a good acquisition or merger. An example of achieving financial synergism is as follows:

The acquiring PDQ Company has earnings of $100,000 and 100,000 shares of stock; this results in per-share earnings of $1. The stock sells for $20 and has a total market value of $2,000,000 and a price/earnings (P/E) ratio of 20.

The acquired XYZ Company has earnings of $50,000 and 50,000 shares of stock for per-share earnings of $1. Priced at $10, the company's stock has a P/E ratio of 10 and a total market value of $500,000.

If there is a share-for-share exchange based on current prices, PDQ Company exchanges 0.25 shares of its common stock for 1 share of XYZ Company. The resulting new company has earnings of $150,000 and a total of 125,000 shares, which comes to $1.20 per-share earnings, or an increase of $0.20. Furthermore, the market price of PDQ Company's stock after the merger might rise to $24, reflecting its normal P/E ratio of 20.

Looking at Earnings From Every Angle

Developing financial goals calls for an evaluation of the earnings of similar kinds of businesses, business cycles, and competition. Overcapacity, of course, can hurt an entire industry and lead to lower margins as has happened in paper. Furthermore, some of the heavy industries and such enterprises as supermarkets and food processing companies traditionally have had low profit margins. The goals would be higher in industries where profit margins and return on investment are higher, as in the pharmaceutical, petroleum, and cement industries.

Another financial indicator for evaluating alternative routes to growth and expansion is profit in relation to total sales volume. However, this can at times be misleading because the profit on sales required to earn a given return on investment varies substantially from one industry to another. Despite this, comparable data on companies should include the ratio of earnings to sales, along with the ratio of return on investment.

The rate of growth of a company and its industry also has a value in determining financial goals. Such growth is controlled to some extent by the availability of funds for investment and by technological developments. Certain new industries seem to have an explosive financial growth and then settle into a more common and ordinary income production curve.

Another financial consideration is the market value of the acquiring company's stock. This is particularly significant if a company intends to use for its acquisition program convertible preferred or common stock. The higher the multiple of market price to earnings, the less expensive is the acquisition, particularly if the company being purchased has a lower market price-earnings ratio than the purchaser.

Setting Realistic Marketing Goals

In the evaluation of marketing strategy and prospects, it is important to consider such factors as product mix, sales force, and the geographical territories in which sales are strong.

In some cases, the marketing goal may be simply to move into new territories. In another situation, it may be to establish manufacturing and warehousing facilities in a new area in order to give the impression that the company is a local industry. In either instance, corporate management may decide that the most efficient approach to the company's marketing goal is via the acquisition route.

Another rather common marketing goal is to obtain a specific share of the market. In some companies, management will proudly claim 3 percent, 10 percent or 20 percent of the market, and here it is possible, if reliable information is available, to set a goal of, perhaps, 4 percent increase per year for the next five years. In some industries, however, reliable information is very difficult to obtain. The U.S. Department of Commerce collects such information, but it is the first to admit that it does not know how many companies there are in certain fields or what share of the market each one or several of them has. Trade associations for all the specific manufacturing capabilities in the United States have some success in gathering data on market share through questionnaires which do not require the company to give its name. However, in most well-operated companies the management has a fairly clear picture of the approximate market percentage the firm enjoys.

In the large consumer goods industries, it is rather common to have as an objective a planned sales increase product by product. Such planning is of great importance to the company because it helps in determining what additional manufacturing capacity will be needed, what personnel must be obtained, and what additional marketing must be accomplished to achieve growth. Product distribution is another very important marketing factor and companies must know very clearly what their objectives are in this area. Often management will look to merger or acquisition to expand its existing distribution network into new geographical areas—overseas, for example—to engage distributors familiar with product lines new to the acquiring company, and to create a distributor network where none exists.

The Paramount Importance of Manufacturing Goals

The objectives in this area determine what the company will produce and what items, if any, will be subcontracted. Some companies manufacture only a few component parts of a product, and purchase the rest needed for the final assembly.

In this area, the level of utilization of facilities is an important consideration. The goal normally would be to make the optimum effective and economic use of capacity and, when a certain percentage is reached, to install new manufacturing facilities.

Manufacturing is also governed by inventory policies and delivery cycles. For example, druggists now call for drugs and pharmaceuticals on a few days' notice rather than on a few weeks' basis as had been common for many years. Thus, the problem of finished goods inventory becomes much more important to the manufacturer. Every effort must be made to move goods faster and thereby cut down on the need for warehouse space for inventory.

In this context, acquisition-minded companies would look to acquisitions that would add immediate or future manufacturing capacity. This might be a company in the same business, or one in an unrelated business but with equipment that could be used as is or adapted to the purchasing company's needs. And the search in this connection need not be limited to equipment. Often the acquiring company will be on the lookout for a company with personnel that can be exchanged in emergencies.

The term "resources interchange" can be used to sum up the manufacturing goal. Simply put, it is the ability of the prospective acquisition to provide personnel, equipment, and manufacturing facilities to augment the existing facilities of the acquiring firm, or to assist the company during periods of abnormal or unexpected manufacturing demands.

Why Research and Development Goals Can be Difficult to Set

Definite relationships have been established between growth and research and development expenditures. The percentage of the sales dollar to be spent on research varies from industry to industry; the greatest users of research and development are companies closely geared to technological advance, such as the petroleum, chemical, and pharmaceutical companies.

One of the problems of establishing research and development objectives for smaller companies with varied product lines is that development and engineering usually are called research; it is difficult to sort out what is really pure or basic research and what is developmental in nature.

Buying R & D Strength

The merger and acquisition-minded company must analyze its research and development goals to determine whether improvement or greater effort in this area is to be a consideration in selecting an acquisition. For example, the company that finds itself falling behind the competition for lack of adequate R&D will want to improve its efforts in this area, either from within, or by purchasing other companies. If the R&D goal is considered paramount, and if the acquisition route is selected, emphasis must be placed on those prospects that have an outstanding R&D record.

Normally, the acquisition would be in a related manufacturing field so that the purchased company's past efforts would have maximum application and the acquired personnel would have at least a basic understanding of the acquiring company's R&D needs. Fortunately, this is a two-way street. Often, smaller firms with outstanding R&D facilities and personnel will be quite weak in, say, marketing or overall management know-how. For such a firm, a merger with or sale to a more "rounded" and well-managed company will mean salvation and greater profits for both parties. Acquiring management, however, must be prepared to wrestle with the acquired management over the relative importance of R&D to the corporation's overall plans and expenditures and the need to keep basic or "pure" research in line with applied or "practical" research.

Community Relations Considerations: A Six Point Program

In this area there has been a growing awareness of the need for corporate interest in the community—meaning not only the local community but also state and national governmental circles and the world at large. Many firms in the last 20 years have shown a great interest in this area and have formulated policies and objectives for employees and company alike for the conduct of relations with local, state, federal and foreign governments.

Most larger corporations today have community relations personnel who evaluate charities, help satisfy local educational and recreational needs, provide jobs for hard-core unemployed, support local organizations, and work with governmental agencies and trade associations.

Having established corporate objectives in this area, the problem, which is a very difficult one, is to combine them into a meaningful policy statement or set of rules that can aid in planning an acquisition program. It is not enough to say that the company wishes to grow to improve its cash flow, obtain new products, and utilize tax loss carry-forward. Rather, it is important that the company have a body of principles or premises that has some meaning when management and the board of directors begin to shape an acquisition policy.

To illustrate the importance of the objectives discussed above, consider the six-point policy statement of objectives of one company regarding its acquisition program:

1. This company wishes to acquire others which are profitable. It is not in the

business of rehabilitating lost causes or losing companies, primarily because there is no reservoir of management talent and it must seek a profitable company under its organizational set-up.

2. The company to be acquired must be well managed and the management willing to remain. This is a natural concomitant of the first statement and mergers must stand or fall on these two very important points.

In many cases, particularly among the smaller public and private companies, the acquired management is willing to stay, especially if the purchase includes a contingency to be earned on profits during a future period of, say, three to five years. Other managers may not be willing to remain for an extended period of time, but they may be willing to continue until a management team can be developed. One way to avoid a mass exodus of managers is to offer a five-year employment contract, which is rather normal in this sort of situation. Such a contract usually calls upon the president to remain for two years after the acquisition as the active head of the firm and for the following three years as a consultant. This provides a breaking-in period and alerts the president of the acquired company to the necessity of finding a top man either within his company or on the outside. Quite often the president has two or three people in mind and once he realizes that he has two years remaining, he can do a forthright job with the advice and help of the top officials of the acquiring company.

3. This company wishes to acquire others in the packaging machinery, light industrial machinery, valves, automatic products, and similar light industrial fields. As a disclaimer, it wants no part of heavy industry, mining, textiles, or foods. (This may sound as if the company has a negative attitude, but, on the other hand, the statement helps emphasize the areas in which it does wish to expand.)

4. The company prefers to purchase companies which manufacture products sold to other manufacturing companies. This does not eliminate the possibility of the acquisition of a compatible company in the consumer goods field. (Here again it may be argued that this limitation is too severe because a consumer goods company could offer many advantages.)

5. This company prefers acquisitions in the Boston-Chicago-Atlanta triangle. (Geographical location of the acquired company is important because inaccessibility would require additional travel and could impair the relationship and communications with the newly acquired company.)

6. The company looks for others doing a gross business of between \$3 million and \$30 million (net worth will probably be in the range of \$1.25 million to \$8 million). If it sees a company with a sales volume of even \$750,000 which could be made a division in one of its companies, it would be interested.

The exclusion of companies below \$3 million is based primarily on the fact that many smaller companies usually do not have a well-rounded management because of the tendency to have a good manufacturing man and a good sales manager but to be deficient in the financial area. The smaller company's profits often are not really sufficient to warrant the employment of a higher-caliber financial man. However, small companies doing business of $500,000 to $1 million are not overlooked in the acquisition planning and screening stage since, in some cases, they may be very valuable additions not as divisions or subsidiaries but as part of an existing product line or operation.

The Fine Points of Screening

The above six-point program is one that can be utilized by almost any company, whether in light or heavy industry. It is also useful for industries which have been excluded such as food, mining, and textiles. With a policy statement of objectives along the lines of the above, it is then appropriate for the company to begin the screening of potential acquisitions.

In the screening process, it was inevitable that the computer would be used in acquisition planning. Originally the computer was viewed as a tool that would do the conventional analyses much faster than the human mind. However, the capability of the computer has led to the development of new analytical approaches that provide answers to questions not formerly raised because of the excessive and costly calculations required. One great advantage of the computer is its ability to screen long lists of possible merger partners before the best candidates are analyzed in depth. The computer also can consider a number of financial and nonfinancial topics and can examine a variety of alternative exchange packages involving stock and cash and variations of the two. Such computer screening, if done in house, is, of necessity, limited to companies with knowledge in the use of such computers and with staffs capable of providing the necessary details. However, it is possible to purchase "made-to-order" computer runs which screen prospective acquisitions from a list of several hundred companies according to criteria selected to suit a particular situation. Thus far, this new use is just beginning, but in time the larger and more ambitious companies in the acquisition field will certainly turn to computers, at least to screen potential candidates and provide in-depth evaluation of top prospects.

Who Should Sift The Facts

What sort of organization is required for a merger and acquisition program? Usually the president of a company takes a great interest in this activity. It has been shown repeatedly that acquisition contacts are best made on a chief executive to chief executive level. In some cases, the president handles the detail as well as the policy determination, but in the larger companies acquisition teams are formed to take part in the planning function. On occasion, a task force may be assembled on a part-time basis from within a company's management to do the planning and to evaluate situations in the acquisition fields. Considerable staff work is needed for planning, assembling, and evaluating information about acquisitions, and opinions have to be solicited from competitive fields, from legal, tax, marketing, finance, accounting, production, procurement, and scientific personnel. The relative importance of these various specialties will depend upon the nature of the company to be acquired and the skills available within the acquiring company.

Today there is ample opportunity for management to study acquisitions and mergers in business schools and at the numerous seminars conducted throughout the year by associations, investment houses, and specialty groups with particular interests in this field. Moreover, there is a growing body of literature on the subject, and daily newspapers and periodicals present day-to-day case studies of immense value to the planning and acquisition group within the company. On occasion, companies new to the acquisition "game" tend to over-organize and to bring together too many people who only get in each other's way. This pitfall can be avoided by having the acquisition handled by a few people operating closely under the chief executive of a company.

Putting Goals to Work

Acquisition-minded companies with clear-cut corporate goals and prepared to make their own acquisition studies have developed various techniques that produce rewarding results.

One highly successful and thorough technique involves the use of a merger and acquisition evaluation chart which is designed to accomplish the following objectives:

1. To make sure that all important characteristics of the potential acquisition are thoroughly investigated;
2. To enable acquisition study teams to standardize their approaches and method of reporting;
3. To require study teams and corporate officers who make the final decisions to put their opinions on a numerical basis;
4. To enable the company to rank, on a continuing basis, all the companies it has ever evaluated.

The evaluation process gets under way when the company hears of an acquisition possibility from one of its many sources—often a trade magazine, people in the industry, product catalogs, and small firms that supply it with goods and services. Preliminary information on the prospect is easy to come by, usually by writing to the company's secretary with a request for recent annual reports, product bulletins, and related information.

Armed with the preliminary information, a corporate planning and development committee begins its assessment. Study teams consider the prospect from a variety of approaches and apply the acquisition and merger evaluation chart in a rough sort of way. After this preliminary evaluation, a prospect may be eliminated but rarely can one be determined a sure bet.

Checkpoints

Prospects that survive this initial screening are visited by corporate officers, after the prospect is advised that the company is interested in acquisition or merger. If the prospect is cooperative, the acquiring company can make a full-scale evaluation using the chart.

The chart calls for consideration of 16 factors relating to any possible acquisition. A financial study team probes about half of these and a marketing study team probes a like number. The factors investigated are the following:

1. *Adaptability.* This is probably the most important of all the factors and deals with the prospect's adaptability to the acquiring company's goals and plans. Is the company doing a creditable sales volume? Are company managers willing to work for a new "boss"? Based on the answers, the prospect is rated on a scale ranging from a low of 3 to a high of 10. The base figure of 3 is used because it is assumed that to have gotten this far the prospect has some adaptability.

2. *Sales and Marketing Setup.* The study team checks at least 12 points, including what products the prospect has brought out in the past five years and how they have fared, what share of the market these products have achieved, what their projected sales figures are for the next five years and how valid the projections are, what customers have bought the products, whether the company is product or customer oriented, whether it sells through agents or directly, whether it has contact with its customers or agents, what impact any outside change—technical or marketing—would have on the company's market penetration, how much the company spent on advertising and promotion in the past three years and in what media, how heavy the turnover has been among its sales managers, how much of its earnings have been plowed back into research and development, and whether top management intends to stay on. The prospect is rated from 0 to 10 on each question, the scores are totaled and divided by 12 to get a final rating.

3. *Past Earnings Record.* A prospect's past earnings are always a primary consideration. A company whose recent earnings have enabled it to obtain a 60 percent return

on investment gets a rating of 10; a company that has broken even gets a 4; and a company with a loss gets a rating of from 4 to 0, depending on the size of the loss.

4. *Tax Loss Carry-Forward.* This is an important consideration since, according to some acquisition specialists, failure of a company to provide tax losses that can be carried forward is one of the most common reasons why acquisitions and mergers fail. However, if a company were to purchase another primarily for this reason, it probably would be buying it for the wrong reason.

5. *Financial Rating.* This factor involves a number of considerations and the study team checks at least 20, including net worth, return on net worth, net profit, cash flow, working capital, and credit lines. A single rating is awarded with a sound company getting 10 and a not so sound prospect getting 3.

6. *Price-Earnings Ratio.* If the P/E ratio is too high, the acquiring company probably would have to pay more than it should. A top rating of 10 would go to the prospect with a very good ratio.

7. *Possibility of Unexpected Increase in Development Costs.* There is always the possibility that the company might make a mistake in assessing the prospect and that it would take more money to put the acquisition on its feet than was originally planned. If the study team feels that such a development would have little impact on the purchaser, the prospect is given 10 points. Expectations of a greater impact would cost the prospect points.

8. *Size of Cash Outlay Required.* A company that would require no cash outlay would get 10 points, and so on down the scale.

9. *Position on the Growth Curve.* Most companies have a growth pattern that resembles an elongated "S" and once a company reaches the top of the "S," its growth is apt to level off for a while. Companies that are beyond the low point of the "S" but have not yet reached the high portion get the highest mark. Thus, the curve has its greatest values near the middle of the "S."

10. *Status of Competition.* If the prospect has no competition, it gets 10 points. Many competitors, all of which are weak, would net 5 points, and many competitors, all of which are strong, would net the prospect a zero.

11. *Industry Outlook.* The prospect's industry outlook is projected for the next five years and this projection is compared with those of the leading investment houses as a check. Prospects of strong growth would give the company 10 points.

12. *Product Outlook.* Not only should the general industry growth prospects be good, the prospects for existing products should also be good. A firm in an industry with an excellent product outlook would get 10 points.

13. *Product Protection.* Will the purchaser get protection for its own products and services by virtue of the acquisition? Will it pick up patents and copyrights of

competing products? Will it gain increased know-how, as well as technical and other skilled personnel? And, if some persons leave the company, will they agree not to compete with the purchaser for at least a few years? Some measure of protection for all of the acquiring company's products and services would net the prospect 10, while protection for most would be worth 6 to 8 points.

14. *Top Management.* How well managed has the prospect been in the past? Has it stayed abreast of the state of the art in its industry? Has it been responsive to the market place and the needs of its customers? How well managed is it today and how well is it planning for the future? Finally, are the top managers the purchaser's kind of people? Values from 1 to 10 are set, depending on the relative importance of each question to the purchaser. Then an average is taken for a single point total.

15. *Resource Interchange.* If both people and equipment could be exchanged in times of stress, the prospect gets 10 points. If only people could be exchanged, 7 points are awarded, and if only equipment could be exchanged, the firm gets 5. If nothing could be exchanged, the firm gets 3 points on the theory that there could be some minimal transfer.

16. *Financial Control.* Since most companies prefer to obtain majority control, firms in which 51 percent could be acquired would be given 10 points.

Each of the 16 factors must be weighted for importance by the acquiring company and the point score for each factor multiplied by its weight value. The final total is the prospect's score.

Obviously, the merger and acquisition evaluation chart cannot make the firm's acquisition decisions for it, but the 16 factors do provide management with an in-depth evaluation of the prospect and its industry. The chart, or a similar technique, is a tool for keeping company goals in focus and acquisition prospects in tune with company goals. The final decision is up to management.

The question often arises as to where acquisition and sale possibilities come from. This topic will be discussed at length in the following chapter.

Chapter 3

MIDDLEMEN: PICKING A TEAM OF WINNERS

Companies in an acquisition mood soon find that their intentions have become known to the fraternity of investment and commercial bankers, consultants, business brokers, and certified public accountants who serve as middlemen, or a sort of marriage broker, by bringing companies together and easing the way to the "altar." The company looking for an acquisition for the first time should acquaint interested investment houses and investment bankers with its interests and goals, although the question of employing an outsider for this important task is a major decision for management. It should be added that often the initial approach will be made by the middleman firm itself with an offer of its services for a fee plus commission in the search for suitable acquisitions.

Advice to Newcomers

Aside from the novice company, is it wise for a concern to take advantage of these services? Actually, it comes down to a matter of personal choice, but the acqusition-minded company will very probably find that it has almost too many opportunities to evaluate adequately once the word is out that it is actively in the market. A prudent first step, then, might be to call the company's growth objectives and criteria to the attention of a middleman who actively seeks acquisitions as a business. His assistance can be useful and desirable. Acquisition and merger search is a full-time business for many of these people; they are knowledgeable, and they bring to the problem an objective viewpoint that can be of great help to the company's management and board of directors.

Proceed with Care

Using a middleman can be tricky, however, and you should proceed with care. In one case, a corporation that was interested in making its first acquisition employed a small management consulting firm with experience in the acquisition field. The company's board of directors and management developed a set of company objectives and a policy for acquisition, which the middleman firm used to line up a succession of potential acquisitions. It soon became evident, however, that the outside consultants had one great difficulty: not having been members of the acquiring company's management, they were not familiar with the practices and methods of the company for which they were working. Such a "gap" can lead to wasted time and energy, and clearly illustrates the importance of a specific definition of needs by the acquiring company, as well as a complete understanding by the middleman of the purchaser's goals. It is appropriate to note that the middleman, after all, is trying to earn a fee, and he is therefore anxious to see a deal made. For this reason, he may be an eager advocate of a particular merger even though the union might not be proper for the two companies involved.

Finders: the Pros and Cons

Finders are independent middlemen who help bring companies together to talk over merger and acquisition possibilities. Corporate executives say that, at their best, finders play a useful role in the growth of companies of all sizes. At their worst, they are, executives say, a nuisance, hounding management with hollow proposals to buy or sell some business activity. "The kindest thing I can say about finders is that they are promoters," is the way one executive put it, while another summed up his views by saying, "Finders merely make introductions and don't help bring the acquisition to a conclusion."

Most finders decline to discuss their methods of operation, but it is a known fact that the nucleus of their operations is the "little black book" (or several dozen of them for each finder) filled with the private phone numbers of corporate executives. Frequently, the approach is a phone call, sparked by a newspaper item announcing a cancelled merger, with the offer of a "far better prospect."

Understanding Finders' Fee Structure

The subject of fees is a touchy point with most finders, probably because they sometimes have difficulty collecting. In one dispute, a Milwaukee finder, William J. Schaller, sued Litton Industries, Inc. for breach of contract, claiming that Litton failed to honor an oral agreement to pay him $521,811 as a fee for his part in helping Litton acquire the Louis Allis Company. Litton countered that the claim was without merit.

Finders also claim that fees are sometimes cut without their knowing about it until it is too late. One finder said that his fee was cut simply by his client listing a smaller fee in the prospectus. Then, too, there is the possibility that shareholders may wade into a fee dispute, challenging payment of what they consider to be an exorbitant amount. In early 1968, for example, shareholders of Glen Alden Corporation filed suit in a New York State court in an effort to block payment of a total of $8 million in fees to four finders. The fees concerned the acquisition by Glen Alden of Stanley Warner Corporation and the purchase of a major interest in Schenley Industries, Inc.

But despite such disputes, it is not unusual for a finder to have a longstanding relationship with certain companies and, without question, finders do have a role to play in mergers and acquisitions.

Doing Business with the Right Business Broker

Business brokers as a group perform a very useful function in the merger, acquisition, and sale of corporations. As the tempo of acquisition has increased, more able and successful men have entered the business brokerage field. The good ones among them are expert at analyzing companies and understanding their needs.

Business brokers, unfortunately, vary significantly in ability; there are even some "ambulance chasers" among them. When considering a deal with a business broker who is unknown to you, it is advisable to look the firm over carefully and to investigate the situation thoroughly. For example, the acquisition-minded company may even receive unsolicited letters from a finder or broker volunteering his services in the search for a suitable company to buy. Such letters are usually vague and imply that the writer is empowered to act in a prospective seller's behalf, although, of course, no specifics are mentioned. This is what might be called the "needle-in-the-haystack" approach, and it is quite likely that the broker or finder does not have the authorization of a company president to approach your company, and that no discussion of fees has been had with the potential seller. Such letters are probably fishing expeditions and if the president of an acquisition-minded company is so foolish as to indicate an interest without establishing certain ground rules, the business broker then has in hand a letter which he can take to a prospective seller and say, "I've got a buyer; now let's get together on fee and I'll get to work on the details."

In replying to such indiscriminate letters, it is important to establish quickly that the acquiring company requires a letter authorizing the finder or broker to act as an agent of the selling company and confirming that fees will be paid by the seller.

Fortunately, the capable business broker is quite ethical. He realizes that his strength lies in his honesty and above-board dealings and that in the long run it is better for him to lose an occasional quick sale than to risk any chance that either the selling or acquiring company presidents will have cause to regret their association with him.

August 19, 1970

Mr. A.C. Mann
608 South Street
Los Angeles, California

Dear Mr. Mann:

In response to your August 3rd letter, I am sending a statement of our acquisition policy.

I should emphasize that we do not pay acquisition fees to brokers since we expect the seller to do that as is common in the real estate market. Also, we would like to have a letter from the president of the selling firm confirming that you are his agent.

I should mention to you that our West Coast group may be calling you about your suggestion. We would like to know whether the machine is available for inspection, when it might be convenient to see it, and would like to get a list of the patents involved.

Sincerely,

William H. Baumer
President

October 6, 1970

Mr. Paul C. Jones
Jones Company
Craig Road
Los Angeles, California

Dear Mr. Jones:

Our acquisition interests do not include electronics and electrical goods nor are we interested in the restaurant field.

Basically we like manufacturing companies, packaging machinery, companies turning out durable goods such as automotive parts, and the like.

I am enclosing a copy of IGI's annual report which will give you some idea of our interests.

I should mention to you that we do not retain brokers for finding acquisitions but confine ourselves to dealing only with brokers who represent a selling company.

Sincerely yours,

William H. Baumer
President

Enc.

Establishing Equitable Fees

It is natural that companies considering their first acquisitions would be concerned about fees to be paid to the middlemen. The question should be raised at the outset, long before any discussions with prospective sellers. A good practice to follow is to leave the fee to the seller. This is the usual practice in real estate deals and has the added advantage in the industrial field of establishing responsibility where it properly belongs. This practice protects against potential dangers that arise when the owner of a business or a large stockholder, while on the golf course or at a cocktail party, says in jest, or half seriously, that he is ready to sell his company. Quite possibly someone who has overheard the conversation will call another company and say that so-and-so is ready to sell. He may add, "I'll be glad to handle the deal." Nothing may develop at that time but a year or so later the company may be sold and the "eavesdropper" who first passed the word along may feel that he is entitled to a fee, even though he may not have participated in the later negotiations. It is to be assumed that the fee will be in the sales price and that the buyer knows he is paying it.

At this point, it is important to note a major distinction between a "finder" and a "broker." A finder, in effect, is a broker of sorts, but he is generally defined by law as one who introduces parties and does not get involved in the negotiations between the parties. A broker, by way of contrast, not only brings the parties together, but participates in the negotiations. Some states permit a finder to collect a fee even when no written agreement exists, but deny a broker this right unless there is a written document stating the commission to be paid.

What about the amount of the fees? There is no stated list of fees that is accepted *in toto* throughout the world of mergers and acquisitions. Some business brokers speak in terms of 5 percent on the first $1 million of the sale price, and then a scale-down of 4 percent, 3 percent, 2 percent, etc. for each additional million dollars. For a $5-million deal the fee would therefore be $150,000. Another way of expressing it would be to say that the fee should be 5 percent of the first million and 2 percent or 3 percent thereafter. In the larger deals it is usually a subject for negotiation. In addition to fee, it is also important that any agreement authorizing a middleman to act in your behalf specify a time limit, usually 6 to 12 months, subject to extension by mutual consent.

Smooth Dealings with Investment and Commercial Banks

Investment bankers have long considered mergers and acquisitions a major part of their business and can prove a useful source of information about particular companies. Furthermore, an investment banker may be able to provide additional services toward the consummation of an acquisition beyond those which a business broker can offer. For example, where there is a public issue of stock or a loan required, an investment firm can help by advising and assisting in the negotiation of terms involved in any financing arrangement. Investment banking firms can also place securities privately with institutional investors, and many investment banking houses have a department specializing in private financing and are in frequent contact with various institutional lenders. They are likely to be of much more use in determining the worth of an enterprise that is being bought or sold and in conducting the negotiations than the business brokers. As a matter of fact, most business brokers who bring in a sale or an acquisition are usually excluded from the dealings thereafter, even though they are paid their fee for bringing the parties together. Investment bankers can play a useful role also during merger discussions by giving advice on the structure of the deal. Since they may be primarily interested in earning a fee, these advisers must be dealt with carefully, but their advice can be helpful, particularly to the novice.

Negotiating With Commercial Banks

The big commercial banks are getting involved in mergers and acquisitions also. In fact, commercial banks have long been involved in this field in an informal way, but in recent years they have set up departments to make matches for their corporate customers. The theory is that one plus one will almost make two; it never makes more in this sector of the bank's business.

In recent years this activity has become so important to commercial banks that at last count there were some 25 banks with departments specifically organized to search out partners for customers or prospects and to advise them on such matters as merger terms, financing, and other related areas.

Pinpointing Bank Problems

One problem the banks face is the shortage of prospects for acquisition. Chase Manhattan Bank and First National City Bank, New York's two largest, have lists of well over 1,000 companies anxious to make acquisitions, while their lists of sellers number only a couple of hundred, not all of them desirable.

At Chase Manhattan it is the corporate finance and research department that acts as a clearing house for mergers and acquisitions for customers. This department works closely with two other departments, financing development and technical services, both of which add their expertise to corporate planning.

Commercial bankers have concluded that unless they aggressively seek merger and acquisition business, they will end up with sellers that have been unsuccessfully trotted around the markets already. For this reason, some banks, such as Chase Manhattan, are starting to ask investment bankers to split fees. However, most commercial banks still look for compensation solely from the new banking business that results from an enlarged company. When a fee is involved, the commercial bank receives it after the merger is consummated; it shies away for legal reasons from putting the fee on a percentage basis.

Working Harmoniously with Certified Public Accountants

Accounting firms have the same basic interest in mergers and acquisitions as banks: both are loathe to lose a client as the result of a merger, and hope to gain business by helping their clients to make acquisitions.

During acquisition or merger negotiations, the buyer's accounting firm usually conducts a purchase audit of the prospective seller's books to make certain that the two accounting systems are compatible. Of late, however, an increasing number of clients are asking the accounting firms to express a disinterested opinion on the pros and cons of the marriage. In fact, some big CPA firms have even generated their own lists of companies for sale, and many accounting firms have set up trouble-shooting departments to handle merger and acquisition work. Despite this trend, however, most CPAs see themselves as catalysts and expect the buyer to handle his own technical examination. Such firms can be helpful in working out the values and establishing exchange ratios.

"More and more businesses are coming to us for consultation and advice because they know we have no axe to grind," according to James Gram, who has been active in merger and acquisition work for the big CPA firm of Touche, Ross, Bailey & Smart. "The XYZ company has A, B, and C divisions, let's say. C's division manager is pushing hard for an acquisition. The president of XYZ may think the world of C's manager, but he may also wonder whether the man's prime motive may not be to increase his own importance within the firm. So he'll come to us for an objective opinion as to whether the acquisition will benefit the firm as a whole."

Of course, this kind of work puts the CPA into the once-private hunting ground of the management consultant, who also bases his pitch on the objectivity of his advice.

Thus, responsible middlemen include the finders, business brokers, investment bankers, commercial bankers, CPAs, and the consultants previously mentioned. Another source of possible buyers and sellers are the ads in such publications as the *Wall Street Journal,* and *Barrons* and the numerous merger periodicals which have sprouted in recent years.

The Role of Suppliers and Customers

Suppliers and customers can also supply leads on companies that either are acquisition- minded or anxious to sell. These men oftentimes do not understand the full import of the information they have, nor do they know exactly where to turn, but they can be very helpful as middlemen. Another source of information is conversation with fellow board members. The president of a company who is on the boards of other companies can tell his associates of his company's interest in acquisitions or sale and may pick up some very useful leads. Sometimes a board member of a company that has considered and rejected a potential acquisition can supply that information to a friend with whom he serves on another board and thereby open up a new possibility. In one such situation, a director was party to an acquisition search which, on the basis of a marketing survey and audit, proved the company in question to be a good candidate. However, the director's company's cash position was such that it could not complete the deal, which the seller stipulated had to be for cash only. The director was able to mention this very good company to a fellow board member of a third company who was able then to follow up and complete the deal.

Putting Trade Associations to Work

Another area of potential help is the trade association executive. He usually is conversant with what is happening among the member companies, including their desires to buy or sell. He will often, though not for a fee or as a broker, act as intermediary to introduce the acquisition-minded company to a potential seller. His suggestions, as well as prospects from other sources, can be checked out by referring to the prospect's annual report, Standard & Poor tear sheets, and, in the case of privately held companies, a Dun & Bradstreet report.

One problem which exists among most selling companies is that if they are too avid in telling others of their availability, they tend to become shop-worn like merchandise which has too often been on the counter. It is a wise course for a company that is thinking of selling to keep its desires as confidential as possible and to limit those to whom it mentions its availability.

In this field of acquisition and merger, the confidential approach is of utmost importance. Company managements who are thinking of selling or buying for the first time are perhaps fearful in this area and with some reason. It has often happened that when a company was thinking of selling, the morale of some of its executives was lowered. They became worried about the future of the company and figured that they had better bail out before the uncertain future unfolded.

How to Handle Broken Engagements

A middleman can be very helpful in bringing together a buyer and a seller but, as in courtship, the first meetings are of great importance. What is said and how it is said may have a great bearing on whether the sale or purchase is consummated.

Considering the frequent reports in the press of cancelled mergers and aborted acquisitions, one is likely to conclude that nearly as many deals are falling through as are consummated. Actually, the success ratio is about the same as it has been for some time. The plain fact is that more transactions are being entered into than ever before and they are being publicly disclosed at a much earlier stage in the negotiations. The recent imposition of full and prompt disclosure rules has forced into the open merger and acquisition proposals that in the past never would have seen the light of day. The New York Stock Exchange, for example, requires its companies to divulge information about major steps, whether under negotiation or in the planning stage, as soon as they extend beyond a company's top management.

Despite this, it is important to realize that there are a number of reasons for breaking a corporate engagement, reasons to which the acquisition-minded company should give careful consideration. Some major reasons are:

1. *Misrepresentation.* All too often a company will cancel the deal when it finds that earnings, assets, or other information presented by the other party are incorrect. As one experienced hand put it, "A close look at the books reveals some interesting surprises."

2. *Financial.* Announcement of a merger or acquisition may result in a serious drop in the price of the stock of one or both companies. In effect, the financial community is registering disapproval of the transaction and this becomes evident when the stock shoots up sharply as soon as the cancellation is made public. On the other hand, a drop in the price of the acquiring company's stock may be completely unrelated to the merger. In this case, however, the drop forces the company to increase the number of shares to be exchanged to maintain the agreed to purchase price; the deal becomes too costly.

3. *Management Disputes.* Failure of the principals to agree over who will run the new corporate entity, what it will be called, who will get the top jobs, or other related matters are other major causes of broken corporate engagements. It is not unusual that an acquiring company will find, after considerable time and effort, that its operating practices and policies are completely out of line with those of the proposed acquisition. Benefits, expense accounts, retirement policies, all are possible areas of disagreement. And finally, the selling company may come to the conclusion that it will lose its operating autonomy.

4. *Last-minute Reluctance (Shy Bride).* After everything seems locked up and agreed upon, the selling company may back down because the owner is suddenly reluctant to part with his "baby." Or the president decides that he does not want to give up the prestige and perquisites of his position. There are many reasons why the selling principals might get "cold feet" and decide to call off the deal. Unfortunately none is easy to foresee.

5. *Opposition.* The list of proposed mergers and acquisitions that have been called

off because of Justice Department disapproval and threats of antitrust action is lengthy indeed. And, even though qualified approval of a pre-merger notification is received, this is no guarantee that subsequent antitrust action or a restraining order will not be sought once the merger or acquisition is consummated. Opposition can come from within as well. Directors, stockholders, or key company officers may fight the proposed union on the grounds of price, or because of preferences for another merger possibility.

Thus, even though all may go well during the initial courting, there are numerous pitfalls to avoid on the way to the "altar." The wise buyer will beware and, fortunately, experience seems to indicate that if the merger or acquisition is being sought for the right reasons, the deal will go through.

Chapter 4

HOW TO HANDLE THE FIRST MEETING SUCCESSFULLY

Organizing All The Details

In the give and take of merger and acquisition there are many questions asked by buyers and sellers, such as "How in the world do you find companies?" "How long do negotiations take?" or, "How do you negotiate price?" Many other questions occur and about the only way to anticipate them is to examine a typical approach to negotiations.

Assume that a middleman, who might be a finder, broker, investment banker, CPA, or some other person interested in bringing companies together (see Chapter 3), calls and says that he has a company he thinks would fit into your plans. Usually the discussion would cover the company's finances, profitability, and type of business. First, you should request the five-year financial statements, which should be carefully analyzed to determine the company's performance in terms of such pertinent ratios as current assets to current liabilities, return on investment, and earnings on sales volume. The fixed assets, long-term debt, and profits over the past few years will be of major interest, and you will want to examine the profit curve for signs of steady growth or a succession of peaks and valleys.

In a normal year, some 200 firms are thus examined. Perhaps 35 or 40 of these are actually visited and out of that number possibly five receive serious proposals. Surprisingly, no more than one or two end up as acquisitions. Actually, however, there is no reason to be discouraged by the seemingly fruitless time and effort involved, because each company looked at offers an opportunity to learn more about the business and about the prospect's particular segment of industry. The net result is that the acquisition-minded company is better qualified to judge when it does see something that fits into its growth plans.

Check and Triple Check

Continuing with an examination of a typical approach, assume that the financial data received calls for further investigation. This may mean that the company is making a 15 percent or 20 percent return on investment and, hopefully, as much as 8 percent return on total sales. Here there must be caution since industries vary markedly in earnings and companies are in different stages of growth.

Conducting the Plant Visit

Before agreeing to go out and visit a company, it is desirable to obtain all available data. If the company is listed on one of the major exchanges, it is possible to secure Standard & Poor's tear sheets, which give the basic data about the company for a number of years; Moody's also has useful information. There is always the opportunity to discuss the industry generally with the company's trade association to determine what competitors and suppliers think of the company and its kind of business.

A note of caution: during this period the confidential nature of the transaction must be respected by both buyer and seller. For this reason, the name of the company is NOT mentioned; only that it is in a certain kind of business and has sales and earnings within a certain range. With the relevant information in hand, it is then possible to arrange a first meeting. In the majority of cases, the meeting is arranged by the middleman, but on occasion, a direct call to the president of the prospective acquisition may be the best approach.

Usually the meeting starts out with the normal trivialities and then moves into a discussion of the company's business, a little of its history, the problems that confront it, and what its successes have been. During such discussions it is desirable to ask questions about the company's future—what new products management has in mind, what basic and/or design patents are available, and what management really would like to see the company become. During this questioning, and in a tour of the plant, it is possible also to get an idea of what is in the minds of the people who are selling the company. Are they seeking to get a pot of cash, or stock? Do they plan to continue in the management for a short time, or to stay and really run a profitable company for the acquirer?

Setting the Tone

The visit to the plant and with the principals of the company must necessarily be somewhat casual, and yet the acquiring company must seek out the whys and wherefores of the operation. Usually a request to see the premises is gladly granted, but in some cases the company is reluctant to show certain unusual machines or processes, fearing that the acquiring company may pick up some ideas for its own use. There is always the question of mutual confidence, and, therefore, the question of how much is going to be presented. The visitor must look beyond and underneath the remarks that are made, and here a measure of intuition is of great help. Probing questions may be asked in a polite and straightforward manner and some people have a greater capacity for this kind of questioning than others. In no instance should the prospective acquirer get angry or upset or challenge the figures or ideas expressed.

The analogy has often been made that the first visit is similar in many ways to the first date with a girl. The first date may be a happy occasion, it may be light-hearted and gay, or it may be an unfortunate experience. It is possible that after the first visit neither side is interested in continuing the relationship.

The Rewards of On-Site Inspection

A visit through a plant is very revealing. It can be expected that an extra amount of house cleaning has taken place and that a strong effort has been made to present the operation as being efficient and well run. In the walk through a plant it is important to note the relations among the workers and how they respond to the head man. Some observers who have done a great deal of acquisition work of this nature say that a plant visit is much like visiting a person's home. The personality of the "housewife" is in large measure unfolded for the visitor to see. Likes and dislikes and methods of operation are all presented for the observer who has a sharp eye for detail.

In one case, a plant visit brought such a negative reaction that no further work was done on the acquisition. The company was in the automotive products field and had within the previous 18 months moved from an old plant in an urban area into a new plant in an industrial park. The exterior was attractive, the grounds were well kept, and the building was spic and span. Inside, however, was a jumble of machines in seemingly poor condition. The plant lay-out seemed extremely inefficient. When a few questions were asked, the host appeared to want to cover up the details. Conditions and attitudes were such that the acquisition seemed undesirable.

By way of contrast, a plant visit may reveal a very modern, efficient plant, well laid out, a minimum number of people present, and everything running very smoothly. Visitors should realize that industries vary and that in some industries, such as roofing, building supplies, and smelting and forging, the possibilities for strict housekeeping are much more difficult than in, say, a pharmaceutical plant, food plant, or a plant in which there is a premium on excellent housekeeping.

Look and Listen Well

One does not need to be an expert to appreciate efficient plant layout and flow of goods. For example, a visitor would be shocked in this age to see machines still being driven by leather and rubber belts, although one occasionally sees such machines, probably 50 or 60 years old, beautifully kept up and in near mint condition. In a visit to a plant in New England, the machines were in a dark and forbidding basement area, and everything seemed to be jammed together in a most inefficient way. In another plant in New England, the people conducting the plant tour were very secretive. The claim of the existence of "a lot of extra machines" proved to be nothing more than a courtyard full of a fantastic array of ancient, rusty machines, which in the mind of the owner seemed to have some value. In addition, the host made dark references to inventory not on the books and when it was suggested that this could cause great difficulty, it was dismissed with a wave of the hand.

It is not likely that one plant visit will answer all the questions or guarantee that the acquisition will be a good one. On the other hand, it is possible during such a visit to observe the kinds of people who run the operation, their relations with their employees, and their day-to-day approach to conducting an industrial enterprise.

Playing Detective with Finesse

The first approach to acquisition, then, involves the old proverb: one picture (in this case, look) is worth 10,000 words. The physical property, of course, is important, but what is more important is the caliber, the feelings, and the general desires of the management team. Thus, it is wise to probe into the number of persons engaged in management, their backgrounds, and their attitudes; all done in a very friendly and direct way. What are their educational backgrounds, previous experiences, and how do they regard the company?

If the candidate company is privately owned, and two or more partners are involved, it is important to establish through discreet questioning who seems to be the dominant partner. Bear in mind that in many cases the partnership originated with two or three men, one of whom was most likely an engineer and manufacturing oriented while the other had a sales background. Rarely in smaller companies doing several million dollars worth of business is there a first-class financial man. Thus, the observer should not be disappointed if he finds that the prospect's individual executives appear to lack the broad managerial talent and experience normally found in the larger corporations. The initial approach, then, involves a look at the physical facilities, detailed examination of the financial statements and other information, and an evaluation of the management team. Once these basics are out of the way, you are ready to make a more detailed evaluation.

Pinpointing Potential of the Business

Paramount among the factors to be evaluated is the proposed acquisition's potential. A company should not be acquired unless it has a growth potential, or unless its assets—physical, human, and/or fiscal—can contribute to the growth of the acquiring firm. This evaluation involves the competition that the prospect faces, its product lines, its research and development procedures, and its goals. With regard to competition and product lines, it is possible to learn the details of plans management has made for the future. One should realize, however, that expectations of long-range plans and carefully detailed programs often are not realized. Many businesses, particularly those with $5 million to $10 million or less in sales, are absorbed in day-to-day operations; the emphasis is on the problems of the current year. Rarely does management look much beyond the current period and when it does, ideas and plans become rather nebulous. Larger companies, on the other hand, usually have planning groups to work out the details of future operations and growth.

Making Every Minute Count

In a very real sense, the acquiring company is making an evaluation every minute of its visit to the prospect. The visiter should be putting together in his mind a profile of the company he is visiting, and the more retentive his memory the better. Ideally, as soon as he leaves the plant, he should dictate or outline a description of what he has seen. The profile should include the corporation and trade names, principal locations of the plants, and pertinent background information, such as history and corporate relationships.

The profile should also include the position of the company in its industry and some reference to the trends in the industry. Is it an ancient industry which is holding on and perhaps going downhill? Or is it a new and vibrant industry where one new idea or one new product may suddenly permit the company to spurt ahead of its competitors?

It is essential, of course, to determine as early as possible whether the seller's motives for selling include any that reflect unfavorably on the value of the business. For example, the seller may be worried about a competitive weakness not readily apparent.

Sizing Up the Management

The next area for comprehensive evaluation is the management. Also, since during the visit only the officers and key employees were observed, the board of directors should be investigated in terms of background, reputation, and experience. Much of the evaluation of the management team can be based on observations gathered during the plant visit, but this should be supplemented by information from industry contacts, suppliers and customers. It is also necessary to determine whether there is a sales organization, or whether the company depends upon manufacturers' representatives or distributors.

The evaluation of financial information should include a detailed look at items which are not fully understood or which demand information in addition to that presented on the balance sheet. This would include references to pension plans, methods of handling inventory and depreciation, allocations for research, and profit-sharing and bonus plans.

A plant visit will reveal very little, if anything, about a company's reputation. This must be determined from other sources: from present and former employees, suppliers, stockholders, customers, creditors, competitors, distributors, and, when the company has publicly traded stock, from investment bankers and security analysts.

Additional Sources of Information

If the company is listed on an exchange, it is possible to get additional data from business periodicals, public relations releases, presentations by the management to security analyst groups, and many other published sources which treat not only the company itself but the industry in which it operates. Non-company sources of information are particularly valuable for uncovering problems, some of which may be apparent and others which may be well disguised. These may be internal problems having to do with management or with the use of working capital, or they may be external having to do with the acceptance of the company's products and the reputation of its distribution and marketing system. In other words, at this stage of the investigation every factor that might contribute to the success or failure of the proposed merger or acquisition should be considered.

Often, it becomes quite obvious that the executives or owners of a company do not want a visitor to be known as the representative of a potential purchaser. In such cases, it is wise to go under the guise of a visiting financial man to whom the company is looking for additional working capital or loans; it is also possible to appear as a customer or as a friend of the management. In one case a company was very concerned that the visitor, well known in industry as an acquisition specialist, might be recognized by name or by face. To prevent this, a special effort was made to keep him away from several employees who might have known him and he was introduced by his military title, since the company was doing some defense business.

A Question of Intent

The initial approach to a company can be very successful or it can be a complete failure. Much depends on mutual confidence and on the serious intent of each side. Occasionally, firms will send men out to look at companies they have little or no intention of acquiring. Conversely, there are always companies that like to talk to acquisition-minded people just to see what kind of price offer might be forthcoming, or as an exercise in the selling technique. The question of intent may be compounded in some companies–private and public–because the chief executive or controlling stockholder may not know his own mind. He will blow hot and cold; he may spend a great deal of time over several months negotiating the sale of his company and then suddenly cut it off. In situations like this, the only alternative is for the acquisiton group to withdraw politely, requesting that it be contacted if at some future time the company renews its interest in being acquired. Usually in such cases, it is a good idea to put a notation on one's calendar, say 90 days forward, to give a call to the individual to determine whether he has altered his decision. A failure to do this can result in missed opportunities.

Case in Point

A company in the precision-gear field was owned by two brothers who could not make up their minds about selling. They were courted by an acquisition-minded executive who visited their plant, lunched with them, got to know them fairly well, and felt with some confidence that when the brothers made a final decision to sell he would be contacted. But no follow up was made and one can imagine the would-be buyer's chagrin when a few months later he saw in a business newspaper that the precision-gear company had been acquired by someone else.

How to Sell Yourself and Your Product

During a plant visit, the acquisition-minded executive must practice salesmanship. He must sell himself and what his company has to offer; in most instances a firm, soft-sell approach is best. The selling firm not only anticipates certain important benefits from the deal, its management is probably much more conversant with the types of acquiring companies and their methods than was the case ten years ago. The owner-manager, for example, may have read about some of the unfortunate things that have happened when a giant company has taken over a smaller one, completely engulfing the operation–changing the management, marketing methods, and manufacturing system, and so altering the facade of the acquired firm that within a year it was difficult to recognize.

A Bad Start and a Happy Conclusion

One owner group several years ago had had the unhappy experience of dealing with a large acquisition-minded company that had sent in 18 different persons to investigate it. The investigators included auditors, financial men, and engineers, as well as research, marketing and even public relations specialists. The owners and managers of the selling company were fearful that if this was the situation before the acquisition, they could expect even worse afterwards. The owners cut off the negotiations and through an intermediary, an investment banking company, approached another prospective buyer with a reputation for leaving its acquisitions in an autonomous state as long as they were profitable. The second would-be buyer offered the selling company assistance in developing its market and profitability and in expanding through its own acquisition program.

As a result of their previous experience, the owners of this selling company were more than affable and friendly during the first visit by the second prospective buyer. The progress was remarkable and by the end of the session, there was a complete meeting of minds. Discussions had progressed so far that all that remained was to establish the terms of the negotiation.

Go Prepared for Anything

One interesting plant visit involved passing through a picket-line. The struck plant was a tumbled-down, ancient, four-story building along a railroad track in a mid-western city. It was the dead of winter, cold and dreary, and most of the plant windows had been broken. The president greeted the visitor and took him through the plant which was being operated at about 25 percent capacity by salaried workers who were turning out an essential product for the firm's best customers. The president was very outspoken about the labor situation, problems he was having, the violence and other difficulties. He gave a brief history of the company, including the long period during which a number of incompatible product lines and companies were added because of the desires of the various members of the board of directors. He said he had fought against these acquisitions and had gradually sold off the various unprofitable subsidiaries and divisions until he was back to the basic product the company had been turning out for some 80 years. Under the existing circumstances and pressures, the president, the visitor felt, exhibited great courage and considerable poise. He was obviously somewhat harried and the visitor was reluctant to impose on his time. As the visitor was leaving, he turned to the president and asked, "If you were in my shoes would you recommend buying into this company or acquiring it?" The host frowned in disbelief and answered: "I would think you were crazy if you bought this company now."

On the next Monday, when the acquiring company obtained a working-control position in the firm through the purchase of stock on one of the exchanges, the visitor received a telephone call from the president, who was even more surprised than he had been at the conclusion of the plant visit. There is a pleasant epilogue to the story; the company is doing well and the president has proved himself to the acquiring company as a first-class business executive.

Reaching the Hard Decision

A final example illustrates the difficulty in reaching a decision. The visit was to a company producing hard goods. The host, who with his wife was the complete owner of the company, told the visitor of his plans and hopes, conducted him through the plant, introduced him to his associates, and showed him everything he asked to see. That night the visitor was the guest at a very fine party attended by the host's neighbors. The next day at lunch and the following evening, the visitor again wined and dined with local groups. The host obviously was interested in the prospective buyer and wanted to introduce him to the important people in the community. The company was doing relatively well and there was genuine interest on the part of the seller. But despite this, the visitor could not convince himself that this was the kind of company he wanted. It sounds very basic and almost unnecessary to mention, but as a result of the first meetings it is highly desirable that both the buyer and the seller ask themselves this important question: "Is this company the one we are looking for?"

Chapter 5

TESTED PRACTICES AND PROCEDURES IN PROSPECT EVALUATION

A Perceptive Look at Management

Many observers like to say that top management in American industry is not worth its high salaries and that it cannot possibly be as important as it is considered to be. Even if one starts with that premise, the more companies one investigates, the more visits that are made, and the more one contacts top executives, the more apparent it becomes that management is the key element in any company.

Usually the management cornerstone is the president or chief executive himself. The chief executive may not have the sort of personality one would like; he may be blustering, sometimes difficult, perhaps even loud-mouthed, or he may be quiet and reserved. But underneath there has to be a hard, solid ability to understand people, to know how to marry all the elements that go into a successful business, and how to bring about successful results. In most respects, the management team will be a mirror of the chief executive. If he is easy-going and not too worried about the future of the business, then most likely those around him will be of a similar temperament. Even the man who frets in this atmosphere because of his drive to accomplish things in a hurry may have to go along with the general pace and tenor of the business.

Decision Makers Hold the Keys to Profits

A company's management has the opportunity to gain or lose in relation to profits. In some respects, the more restricted and regulated businesses, such as banks and finance companies, have a different kind of executive than the manufacturing or service company. Executives in the former group often are of a mold, and it has been said that even a less than average manager can not do a great deal of harm to the profit situation of a bank or insurance company. The company will not grow and progress under his leadership, but, on the other hand, it will not regress seriously in a matter of a few years. On the other hand, a chief executive in an industrial manufacturing complex can almost make or break the company in a short time. The decisions he makes can in many cases cause tremendous gain or serious loss. The decision to move ahead with certain research, to push for rapid development of a certain product, to change distribution or sales methods, to alter financial policies of the company—all of these can cause substantial fluctuations in the gain or loss of an industrial enterprise. Thus, management knowledge, drive, and motivation are all factors which must be evaluated when looking at a prospective acquisition.

Assuming there has been a visit with the prospect's management, it should be considered a courtship to be followed by other visits. Most acquisitions take several months and during this period one's first reactions to the chief executive and his management team may change radically. Some people make a very good first appearance, but on closer examination, perhaps even involving a budding friendship, they may show qualities that cause one to question their ability to successfully mobilize and direct an industrial operation.

Top-Level Managers: Look for the Creative Spark

The top man must be a formidable individual. And he must bring together a small group of managers who have the attitude and ability to make a company grow. These managers will have certain creative abilities, but probably more importantly they will have the know-how and drive to develop other managers who will produce good products and sell them for a profit.

Fortunately, the excellent or above average chief executive is not of a mold. There seems to be no easily definable managerial type. Some are rough diamonds; others are gentlemen to the core. Some are tough in a quiet, discreet way; others are tough in a hard, blustering way. Most executives who are successful, however, are men of ideas; they are introspective to a certain degree and they have an ability to analyze a situation. But above all, they have the ability to make decisions and to carry them out with energy and dispatch.

By way of comparison, it is worthwhile to consider the course in leadership given at the United States Military Academy at West Point, in which the many types of world leaders are discussed. Examples by name are given and the individual's abilities are evaluated. Inevitably the successful world figure has know-how, the ability to evaluate and analyze alternatives, and he makes decisions and carries them out. It is often said that the successful military leader is the one who, with the information available, makes his decision and, even if the decision is not the best, carries it out with force and ability. This is not to suggest that military leadership and business leadership are synonymous, but there are similarities in qualities and potential of leadership. Industry is highly competitive and it has many experiences in common with the military.

Weighing Managerial Talent

There are evaluation lists available which suggest that the prospect's management be shown by name, age, address, position in the company, background and experience, responsibility, apparent attitude toward the acquisition, and likely post-acquisition position. In addition, such factors as stock ownership, options, pension, profit-sharing, compensation, and relationship to other employees in the company are all part of the evaluation of management.

Some students of acquisition go into each manager's contribution to the business, attitude, importance to the company, and position in the organizational structure of the company. However, it is questionable that this much data is necessary for a meaningful evaluation. The most important individuals are the chief executive and two or three of his assistants. Since a capable top-level team usually will be asked to remain after the acquisition, it is important to evaluate the executive team in terms of its effectiveness and cohesiveness as a top management unit. The character and ability of the members of this unit are more important to a successful post-acquistion situation than the contributions and attitudes of the rest of the acquired company's managers.

Solutions to Financial and Tax Questions

Acquisition-minded companies usually have available a staff of experts in accounting and tax areas who are able to evaluate the statements made by the prospective acquisition. A good accountant will compare the balance sheets and the profit-and-loss statements, look carefully at the asset side of the picture, and make some evaluation of the fixed assets. The major question to resolve is whether the statements show the generation of an inefficient asset pattern. The accountant undoubtedly will question some of the assets, particularly if the fixed assets include old buildings which are heavily depreciated. He may look upon this as an indication of the need for reevaluation, or he may find that these old buildings and the land have appreciated in value far beyond what is shown on the balance sheet. The seller might well consider having a third-party appraise his fixed assets, since his selling price, which is based on net worth, should naturally include the reappraised value of the assets.

"X-Raying" the Financials

An evaluation of a company should include accounts receivable and inventories. The first question should be: How much is the value of the inventory, and what is the turnover? Turnover varies substantially from industry to industry; in some businesses it may be eight times a year, in others only two or three times annually. Accounts receivable should always be checked for age and grade, reserves carried for losses, and the amount of expected losses. This would lead next to an evaluation of the debt policies of the company. The acquirer should always secure all relevant data on long-term debt and any unusual relationships between the creditor and the company. Information should be collected on prepayment clauses and interest rates, and special attention should be given to maturity dates and plans for paying off the long-term debt. The other important item under current liabilities is accounts payable. Much can be discovered about a company by seeing the age of these accounts and the company's policy for handling its month-to-month accounts payable.

The financial evaluation will take into account the net worth of the company, both as shown on the balance sheet and under a possible reappraisal of the fixed assets. It will take into account the return on investment and other ratios, such as the return on total sales. Even more important is a graph of the trend over the past five or ten years for earnings per share, net income or loss, ratio of current assets to current liabilities, and reduction or accumulation of long-term debt.

Looking Behind the Profit and Loss Statement

The above considerations are usually second nature to the acquiring company and probably are more easily handled than almost any other part of the evaluation of the prospect. The trick is to look behind the figures and to discern the growth potential and the possibilities for continued growth in the light of competition in the industry. It is necessary to look at the people, the purchasing methods, and the marketing set up. Particularly if the company is selling a product, which is more often the case, the next area to look into, and far more difficult to analyze, is that of marketing.

Evaluating the Marketing Effort

The initial investigation into a company's marketing program should reveal how many salesmen there are, if there is a sales organization, the number of manufacturing representatives and how well they have done over the past few years, the wholesale distribution network if there is one, and future plans. Some smaller companies depend upon manufacturing representatives, and when their sales grow to $4 or $5 million annually, they begin to develop a marketing organization of their own. This is easier said than done and requires a great amount of ability and time. An efficient nationwide sales force is one of the most difficult organizations to put together.

In looking at one company with a nationwide sales organization of approximately a dozen persons, it was found that two men were very strong in the midwest and eastern areas, but in the west one ineffective salesman after another had worked for the company. The fault might have rested with the company itself, which because of its eastern seaboard location gave very little supervision and sales service.

The market for a company's products should be examined very carefully. Some companies by the nature of their business are confined to a limited territory. This is particularly true of forging and smelting companies and building product manufacturers, for which long-distance freight rates make distances of more than one night's freight run unprofitable. Other companies with nationwide sales forces will find that their products have greater acceptance in some areas than others. This may relate to the varying abilities of the salesmen, different degrees of competition, or the desires and needs of the people in certain areas.

Analyzing the Total Marketing Plan

Here again, the acquiring company may work up an analysis of the marketing program and organization. The marketing plan can be described and an effort made to establish the basic marketing strategy. Particular attention should be paid to any significant changes which have been made in the plan, such as the replacement of manufacturing representatives by salesmen, since this will have some influence on sales volume. The marketing plan of the company should be compared with that of the competition, particularly regarding the discount structure, incentives, cash discounts, and all the other elements in the marketplace.

The product lines should be described and each product examined to determine how it is sold and if it has a relationship to other products. The ratio of sales of each line to total gross sales should be established and graphs made of the sales of various products. In most companies there is no fixed ratio and a new product may start slowly and overtake old products. Johnson & Johnson used to say that of all the products it had, the new ones and the more glamorous ones did very well, but in the last analysis it was always pleasant to see how just plain cotton and gauze sold in the marketplace.

Marketing: The Multi-faceted Tool

In addition to product lines, it is well to look into seasonal sales patterns. A company which manufactures toys or textiles, or women's wear, will naturally have a different seasonal sales pattern than a company in the machinery business. In addition to sales patterns, it is important to examine the cost of physical distribution of the product. The market should be identified and efforts made to secure a list of the principal purchasers over the previous few years. Close attention also should be given to the relationship between civilian and military sales. This relationship may fluctuate in such a way as to cause difficulties for management planning.

The sales structure, salesmen's compensation, sales tools furnished the men, training programs, salesmen's average tenure with the company—these and many other questions should be asked and answered as fully as possible.

Taking a Sharp Look at Manufacturing

An evaluation of manufacturing, including engineering and purchasing, will raise many questions about the company's production methods. Some companies insist that they manufacture all products they sell. Others have a flexibility which permits subcontracting of certain component parts of a product. Some companies put more emphasis on the product assembly than on the manufacture of components that go into the product. The acquiring company must evaluate the basic manufacturing policy of the prospect, the methods used, materials, facilities, equipment, quality controls, and all the other elements of manufacturing.

There should be a great interest in whether the company makes or buys its products, what the proportion is, and how it was arrived at. The approximate mix in dollars and percentages should be determined, as well as who makes the decisions and under what circumstances.

The manufacturing process should be described in terms of the materials used, sources of supply, machines, skills, facilities, and whether there are licenses and patents. For companies which use a basic product, such as ore or cotton, it is important to know when the items are purchased, who handles the purchase, how much money is available, and what are the purchasing demands on the cash position of the company.

The manufacturing facilities should be listed and the value of all pieces of equipment, as well as the cost of the land and buildings (including age and improvements), should be carefully added and included as a part of the overall sales agreement. Similarly, the evaluation should include kinds of equipment, whether custom-built or standard, value, efficiency, age, cost of maintenance and repair, and whether the machines are obsolete.

The coordination of purchasing with other control departments, a review of major critical suppliers and their financial status, and the method of working with them, should also be a part of this evaluation.

Research and Development: Looking at it from all Aspects

The main purpose of the company's research effort should be established and it should be determined whether it is applied or basic. Further, what is the budget for research, how much is for basic research and how much is for development and engineering effort? The importance of research to the company should be analyzed since this varies considerably from industry to industry. The company's record for development of new products, new materials, and new methods should also be reviewed, and there should be an evaluation of research, manufacturing, and engineering personnel.

This leads to a careful look at the working situation. Does the company have a union? If so, what contracts exist and what has been the relationship with the union? If there have been strikes and many difficulties between management and labor, this should be a warning signal indicating the need for close examination of this problem. Area-wide agreement among labor unions should be investigated.

In larger companies the employees may be members of several different unions. The transportation group, the manufacturing group, the office group, may belong to different unions and the timing of contract negotiations can be important to the future operation of the company.

Growth and Competition: How Much, How Soon

Taking into account the financial and tax questions, management, labor, manufacturing, engineering, research, marketing, and all the other functions of the company, the next question logically becomes: What is the possibility for future growth of the company? Before answering this question, the acquiring company must look into the industry itself. This includes its record of achievement, rate of growth, any statistics on what other companies have done, and, particularly, what the competing companies are doing. The question of growth is often a value judgment by the acquiring company. To put all of the factors mentioned above into a computer might produce a gross conclusion having little to do with the future.

The growth of a company is often dependent upon the availability of finances, the caliber of management, technological changes, the development of a new product, and the appearance of new needs among the population. There are so many factors which enter into the growth of a company that it takes a very responsive individual to make a meaningful evaluation.

Let the Buyer Beware

Within the physical plant, among the employees, and in the business field in which the company is operating, there are many considerations which must be evaluated. Those that have to do with federal or state government regulations are left to later discussion. There are, however, a great many small but significant items which should be considered in an evaluation of the company. One of these is the various contracts with customers and distributors, many of which may have rather unusual clauses which seemed perfectly reasonable years before when they were negotiated. Such things as "understandings" with major suppliers should be investigated as far as possible, and guarantees and endorsements examined as another possible source of some difficulty later on. It is assumed that the legal counsel at the acquiring company will look into any encumberances on the property, and that there will be a list of chattel mortgages or conditional sales. There will necessarily be a check of all insurance in force, including life, workmen's compensation, property, liability, title, and others. Major litigation, either pending or resolved, should be investigated thoroughly. Moreover, there may be disputes or claims which have not yet arrived at the stage of litigation, and these should be well known to the acquiring company. Also, it should be ascertained whether there are employment contracts, secrecy agreements, or other covenants about disclosures of information on products and processes. These are only a few of the dozens of items which should be looked into on a subsequent evaluation. Special attention will normally be given to royalty agreements, trademarks, brand names, patents, and copyrights. These will vary considerably, and companies in the consumer goods field will have a great variety and number of such agreements.

Valuation Procedures

There is no neat formula for arriving at a price for a bundle of assets and abilities which the seller is offering. Value cannot be fixed in a vacuum. Rather, the most meaningful evaluation is one put in terms of other opportunities and alternatives open to the purchaser. A sure-fire question is: How attractive is this particular company compared to others which might be found, or with the acquisition of machines and management that could accomplish the same result? In the latter case, the purchaser must also place a value on time. To purchase the company he would have instant production, whereas the creation of a similar capability might take many months and might result in unexpected complications.

Valuation of a company is an analytical and imprecise art. The aim is to establish a price range in which the negotiation may be conducted. The buyer's own judgment is assisted by careful analysis. Three methods of valuation are as follows:

1. *Net worth.* This is the most common starting point. The owner's equity is the value of the tangible assets he is selling. Net worth cannot give a value to good will, to an established position in a market, to the worth of specific products, or to the new products being researched and developed. It can also be misleading since it does not give a true picture of the replacement value of plant and equipment. Thus, the professional purchaser will be willing to bring into the negotiations an appraisal of the fixed assets, or what is commonly called "reappraised net worth."

For many years, companies were bought at figures close to reappraised net worth. In recent years, sellers have become more sophisticated and seek to include in the sales price additional consideration for such general factors as market position, expected new products, and potential growth. As a result, purchase prices have multiplied three or four times in relation to net worth. Also to be considered is the price being paid for the equity. If it is stock being sold on the market at a high price-earnings ratio, the multiple of net worth does not look so awesome. If the sale is for cash, the price offered will usually be closer to the hard value.

2. *Cash flow, return on investment.* This is a relative valuation technique. What should the return on investment be in the seller's company and in the industry in which he operates? The rate of return is useful in evaluating a business that is expected to have a relatively stable pattern of future earnings that will permit excess cash to be withdrawn.

In evaluating one company, the owner asked a figure 20 times earnings and almost three times net worth. His price was $6 million and earnings, which were stable, were $300,000. He asked for preferred stock paying six percent interest. When it was pointed out to him that the earnings would not pay the interest and that there would be a negative return on investment, he realized how unrealistic his asking price was.

3. *Price/earnings multiples.* Sellers are usually aware of the P/E ratios of the purchase prices of other companies in their industry. Accordingly, they will set their price at 20 to 25 times earnings, excluding from consideration the intrinsic value of their company as compared to others in their industry.

Price/earnings ratios are self-evident examples of the importance of relativity in the valuation process. The ratios have importance only in comparison with similar ratios for alternative investments. These ratios are important when there is a public market for the stock of both companies. A company whose stock is selling at 10 times earnings will be understandably reluctant to pay 20 times earnings for a similarly oriented company unless there are other significant factors present. Privately owned companies normally do not command a price/earnings multiple as high as that for an identical company that is publicly traded. This helps account for the number of acquisitions by public companies of others that are traded on a major exchange. The public company can offer a stock that is regularly traded and which will fluctuate with the market.

If future earnings of a company are expected to remain relatively stable, the price/earnings multiple merely represents the rate of return to be anticipated on the investment. On the other hand, many stocks trade at multiples of 20 or 30 because the management expects that increased earnings in the future will bring a greater return on investment. Implicit here is a compelling reason explaining why some purchasers are willing to meet asking prices which are out of line with reappraised net worth and present return on investment.

None of the above three valuation procedures should be used solely in negotiating a purchase. Rather, all of them should be taken into account to define a reasonable range for price negotiations.

A Meeting on Principles by the Principals

After a series of get-acquainted and investigatory meetings between the seller and the buyer, and a fairly thorough evaluation of the company, the time is ripe for a meeting to agree on basic principles. At such a meeting it is desirable, if possible, not to have the middleman or broker present, and it is questionable whether the lawyers should attend. Rather, the meeting might best be handled with no more than two or three principals from each side. These men should discuss reasonably and rationally the problems that have been raised by the evaluation, and reach a gentlemen's agreement on how they will be handled. A meeting of this kind may take several hours, ending with a luncheon or dinner, or it may continue long into the evening. The result of the meeting should be summarized in a letter to the prospect's president along the following lines:

Dear Jim:

First I want to tell you again how appreciative I am of your kindness in coming to visit with us last Monday. To summarize in a nonlegal way what we were talking about, let me say first that we would like very much for you and Wynaco to join the Greatest American Corporation. I know you would be welcome and would add a great deal of capacity to our corporate family.

Specifically our suggestions are: (1) that Greatest American Corp., or one of its affiliates, purchase for cash the assets of the present company, paying therefore the stated net worth, plus an appropriate increase, representing the difference between the carrying value of the machinery and equipment and the true value as determined by a competent appraiser. The appraiser should be chosen by you, subject to our approval. (2) In addition to the cash purchase price, we would pay annually an amount in cash equal to 25 percent of the pre-tax earnings for five years or until the total of $750,000 had been paid, whichever comes first. (3) Included in our purchase of assets we would like to have the use of the present corporate name for our new operating company, which would be formed and wholly owned by the purchaser. (4) The present company would remain the property of the present stockholders with assets consisting of cash and the contingent purchase agreement. Aside from changing its name, we would have no interest in its ultimate disposition. Operating arrangements could be made with the new company to collect receivables of the old company. (5) An appropriate lease would be entered into between the new company and the trustees of the partnership that owns the present buildings and land. (6) We would want your present officers and directors, and particularly yourself, to agree to remain and to serve the new company, hopefully at least until the contingent payment had been completed. We would like to add three members to the board of the new company and these would be people that you met in recent weeks. (7) I have outlined to you the facilities we have to offer our corporate family members: commercial, financing, insurance, fringe benefits, personnel recruitment, tax and data processing advice, and others. I will say to you again it is up to your board to decide which, if any, of these facilities they wish to utilize. (8) It would not be necessary to await the completion of the annual audit on December 31. The down payment could be made subject to adjustment when the final audited figures are available.

I believe the above summarizes the important points in our discussion. The thing I want to emphasize to you as a friend and a possible future associate is that what we are suggesting is the best way to assure the continuity of the very fine institution which you have built, liquidity for the stockholders, security for the employees, growth, and continued service to your valued customers.

In our corporate family are other companies that certainly can be of help to you and to your company. We will do our utmost to assure that their experience and knowledge is available to you at your request.

Let me hear from you further when you are ready.

Sincerely,

The Purchase and Subsequent Negotiation

The negotiations having moved to this point, it is now desirable to proceed to a discussion of how companies are purchased, or how the deal is negotiated. Later on in this book we will discuss the marriages that fail and also more importantly what kills many deals. Sometime earlier both the buyer and the seller have answered the question to their own satisfaction: "Why do I want to buy or sell?" Having crossed that bridge, the next move is to determine the terms. There is a long history of negotiations and acquisitions available to both interested parties. The subject of terms will be dealt with in the next chapter.

Chapter 6

SMOOTHLY NEGOTIATING THE DEAL

Up to this point we have considered the preliminaries. Now comes the trickiest part—the negotiation. It requires complete preparation, a cool head, patience, timing and an understanding of people. It is also the fun part of acquisition and merger since all of one's ingenuity and skill are taxed to the fullest. Each deal is different; every deal is a challenge. In the majority of cases, the buyers have been through other negotiations and know where they succeeded and where they failed. Usually, it is the seller's first negotiation, particularly if he represents a privately owned company. If the sought-after company is public, the buyer may find experience sitting across the table.

Everything in the Right Sequence

Breaking the problem down, there is first the preparation. This involves deciding on the method of purchase, and the strategy to be followed, including the time and place of meetings and the participants to be present. Price and tax considerations must also be planned for. Finally, there is the day of decision, the meeting which hopefully will result in a mutual agreement on price and method of purchase. After that, the details can be filled in by accountants, lawyers and tax counsel. In this chapter there is also a discussion of what kills deals, since this information may prove helpful in actual negotiations.

In the timetable of negotiations for an acquisition, it can be assumed that the normal sequence of events goes this way: (1) a middleman brings the deal to a company, along with sufficient financial data; (2) this is studied by the acquiring company, and after a week or two a decision is made to proceed or to forget the proposition; (3) then arrangements are made for a plant visit and for further meetings, which may span a week or two or a month or so (It is rare that two or three meetings and a plant visit can take place in less than a month); (4) next there is an evaluation of all the functions of the business; (5) finally, the parties meet to establish a basic agreement, followed by the negotiation of the contract. A rough rule of thumb is that it takes about two to three months to reach this point. In fact, some negotiations have gone on for two or three years; they would start, be discontinued and forgotten, and then begin again, going through several such cycles. Probably, such drawn-out negotiations indicated that the deals were not very intriguing, otherwise they would have been consummated on the first go-around.

The shortest negotiating time known to the authors was two hours; others were consummated within three or four days. These, however, are definitely exceptions, since three months from start to finish is a much more likely negotiation period.

Selecting the Best Method of Purchase

In the first chapter it was stated that in acquisitions and mergers, the majority of the deals involved the exchange of stock. Unquestionably, the most accepted vehicle is the "tax-free" stock exchange. This has great appeal for the seller since he pays no tax until he sells his newly acquired stock. If he receives cash for his company, he will have to pay a tax on the capital gains at the close of the current fiscal year. Here again one runs into individual preferences. Some sellers prefer to pay the tax in the current year leaving the net proceeds for other interests. Others prefer to own a stock with growth potential in the hope they can add to their estates a useful bundle of certificates which they anticipate will increase in value.

Before negotiating a deal, the buyer and seller should consider the more common methods of acquiring a firm. The basic purchase media are stock, cash, and debt issues, or some combination. The important criteria are whether the acquisition is a tax-free reorganization or a taxable transaction. The methods of payment or purchase include a variety of devices such as debentures with warrants, convertible debentures, installment payments, earn-out or contingent payments, and guaranteed stock prices. The tax-free approach will be considered first.

The A, B, C, D and E of Tax-Free Reorganizations

The Internal Revenue Code recognizes six types of reorganizations, which are classified as "A" to "F". The "A", "B" and "C" reorganizations deal primarily with corporate acquisitions. The "D" reorganization is a loophole covering provisions applicable to spin-offs. The "E" concerns recapitalization, and the "F" covers changes in identity.

The reorganization provisions of the Internal Revenue Code are complex. Also, for the acquisition-minded executive, there is a complex body of case law and history. Tax advice on any reorganization is a must.

The "A" reorganization is defined as "a statutory merger or consolidation." It can be illustrated as follows:

The X Corporation and the Y Corporation are separate companies. The X Corporation, under state law, is merged into the Y Corporation. As part of the reorganization, the shareholders of the X Corporation exchange their shares of stock for stock in Y.

The X Corporation and the Y Corporation are separate companies. Pursuant to state law, the X Corporation and the Y Corporation are consolidated into a new Corporation Z. The shareholders of X and Y Corporations exchange their stock for stock in Z.

A technical distinction between a merger and consolidation is that a merger involves combining two or more corporations into one of the former independent corporations as the continuing entity. A consolidation involves the combination of two or more corporations into a new corporation organized to conduct the combined former businesses. The merger route is the more customary of the two, but most comments concerning statutory mergers would apply to consolidations.

The Crucial Test: Legality

The essential element to qualify a merger or consolidation for tax-free treatment is that it be statutory, that is, that it be accomplished in accordance with the corporation laws of the state or states of incorporation of the merging companies. The result of the merger or consolidation is the same as the acquisition of assets of one corporation by another corporation, whether for stock or cash, in the realization that post merger, two businesses formerly conducted separately are continued as one corporate entity. However, corporation laws of the states contain important differences between a merger as a method of acquisition as opposed to an acquisition of a corporation's assets for stock or cash.

In most states the procedure for merger is that the boards of directors of the merging corporations must approve a merger agreement setting forth the terms, and then submit the agreement to the stockholders of each of the corporations for approval by the required statutory vote. In New Jersey, for example, the merger agreement must be submitted to a vote of stockholders on 20 days notice. A favorable vote of two-thirds of the stockholders is required to effect the merger. In Pennsylvania, only a majority vote of the stockholders is required to complete the merger.

Both New Jersey and Pennsylvania, as well as many other states, have a statutory method whereby a dissenting stockholder may have the value of his stock appraised by a disinterested referee and be paid its fair value by the corporation.

An acquisition by statutory merger, the "A" reorganization, has a substantial advantage over the "B" and "C" type acquisitions. Later when we discuss the acquisition of assets or stock in exchange for the stock of the purchasing corporation, it will be apparent that the buyer is most often limited to the use of its voting stock to pay for the acquisition. The Internal Revenue Code imposes no such restriction on a statutory merger to attain tax-free status. In the latter case, the consideration for the acquisition may include such securities as preferred stock, debentures, bonds and other classes of securities, limited only by the corporation statutes of the states involved and by court imposed requirements of "continuity of interest." This flexibility in selecting the method of purchase price in an acquisition may overcome difficulties caused by discrepancies in dividend payments.

Advantages of Statutory Merger

In a statutory merger of two companies whose stocks are priced equally or in a multiple, the dividend payments may vary by 10 to 20 percent. In an even exchange between two corporations whose stocks are priced equally but have a difference in dividend-per-share of $1.00 to $1.20, it is possible to increase the package offer through interest or additional stock to satisfy any shareholders who might oppose the merger.

Another advantage of a statutory merger over an acquisition of assets is that title to the seller's properties vests in the surviving corporation by operation of law. No closing documents are required other than the merger agreement filed with proper authorities. Contrarily, in the acquisition of assets, a "C" reorganization, deeds to property must be delivered and recorded, as well as assignments of leases, bills of sale, patent and contract assignments. Also, separate instruments must usually be executed concerning assumptions of obligations. The collections and expense of gathering the above documents could be costly and time-consuming for the acquiring corporation.

A "B" reorganization under the 1954 Internal Revenue Code is concerned with tax-free, stock-for-stock acquisitions. In the merger world they are usually referred to as stock swaps or as exchange-of-stock deals. The Code defines exchange-of-stock acquisitions as follows: "The acquisition by one corporation, in exchange solely for all or part of its voting stock (or in exchange solely for all or a part of the voting stock of a corporation which is in control of the acquiring corporation), of stock of another corporation if, immediately after the acquisition, the acquiring company has control of such other corporation."

Control means the ownership of stock possessing at least 80 percent of the total combined voting power of all classes of stock entitled to vote and at least 80 percent of the total number of shares of all other classes of stock in the corporation.

It is evident that the two major elements in the definition of a tax-free, exchange-of-stock acquisition are that (1) the acquiring company must exchange solely its voting stock for the stock acquired, and (2) must have control of the acquired company immediately after the exchange.

The Corporate Reorganization Route

The acquisition of stock of another corporation by the acquiring firm is permitted to qualify as a "B" reorganization even though the acquiring corporation already owns some of the stock of the acquired corporation. This type of acquisition is permitted tax free in a single transaction, or in a series of transactions, occurring over a relatively short period of time, such as one year.

An often used "B" type reorganization is the so-called earn-out or contingency payment. The purchaser wishes to issue voting stock dependent on the future earnings over a five-year period of the acquired company. The reason for this is that it is not easy to value the acquired business for the purpose of determining the number of shares of stock to be issued. Where the acquired company is a closely held public company or a privately owned company, there is no way to know what earnings the acquired company will generate.

In order to solve the problem, the acquiring corporation will issue a certain number of shares at the time of the exchange, say two-thirds of the agreed number, and will then issue additional shares depending on future earnings. The statutory requirement is that the acquiring corporation must issue the stock within five years. As an example, X Corporation, the acquiring company, offers to exchange its own voting stock for all of Y Corporation stock on a basis of one share of X stock for each share of Y stock surrendered. In addition, if prior to the end of a five-year period, commencing with the date of the exchange, the X Corporation reports an annual net profit in any year of $1 million before taxes, the Y shareholder will receive an additional share of X Corporation stock for each share of Y stock surrendered. As a note of caution, it is wise to spell out how profits before taxes will be determined, since unreasonable expenses such as interest on new loans may downgrade the total profit before taxes. Furthermore, the agreement must state the maximum number of shares to be issued over the designated period, and the agreement to issue stock must be non-assignable.

To qualify as a "B" reorganization, the transaction must meet three judicially imposed requirements as well as the statutory requirements.

1. *The business purpose test.* Generally the business purpose must be to continue the entity as a going business. An acquisition and transfer solely for the purpose of distributing marketable securities to shareholders would probably not meet this test and would be taxable.

2. *The continuity of interest test.* Under the court-imposed concept, the former equity owners of the seller must have an equity interest in the buyer after the acquisition. If the selling shareholders received only bonds in exchange for their stock, they would become creditors, their equity interest would terminate, and the transaction would be taxable.

3. *The step transaction test.* The entire transaction will be considered as a whole and the individual steps ignored. The steps will be considered as a single transaction. If it were not for the step-transaction doctrine, a corporation could acquire part of another corporation's stock for cash, and then shortly thereafter acquire the remaining shares as part of a stock-for-stock exchange. Another possible way to circumvent the stock-swap requirement would be for the acquiring company to redeem its stock for cash shortly after making the stock-for-stock exchange. Any transaction in which cash is given in addition to stock nullifies qualification under the "B" type reorganization.

Tax-Free Acquisition and Merger

The majority of sellers—whether private or public—prefers not to pay any income tax immediately on the sale or merger of their business. They can avoid immediate tax impact by exchanging the stock of their company for that of the buyer. This stock might be either common or preferred. The buyer must make sure that he will receive at least 80 percent of each class of the seller's stock in order to make the transaction non-taxable. The seller may have had a basis or original cost of his stock at $1 a share, which becomes the basis for the buyer's stock received by the seller in the transaction. When the seller disposes of the stock, he will be liable for the usual capital gains tax, just as in the sale of any other marketable security.

The buyer might not like the idea of purchasing stock in the seller's company because he thereby assumes all of the real or contingent liabilities of the company. This can have particular dangers when the seller's company is privately owned. Methods of accounting for inventory, the handling of expense accounts, and many other accounting problems may arise to plague the purchaser. Instead, a buyer may conclude there is a sufficient tax or legal exposure to warrant the purchase of assets only, leaving liabilities and exposures to the seller. He might therefore offer voting stock for the assets of the seller.

The above method of acquisition is referred to as a "C" type reorganization and it is also tax free. The tax law defines this type of acquisition as "the acquisition by one corporation, in exchange solely for all or a part of its voting stock...of substantially all of the properties of another corporation, but in determining whether the exchange is solely for stock, the assumption by the acquiring company of a liability of the other...shall be disregarded."

The tax-free, stock-for-assets reorganization involves two major requirements. First, subject to certain qualifications, the medium of payment for assets must be voting stock of the buyer. Second, the buyer must acquire substantially all of the assets of the seller. The Internal Revenue Service ruled that the buyer must acquire substantially all the assets, either at 90 percent of the fair market value of the net assets, or 70 percent of the fair market value of the gross assets. The seller under this arrangement can liquidate the old company and pass the stock received from the buyer to his own shareholders.

As in the stock-for-stock acquisitions, the same three tests of business purpose, continuity of interest, and the step-transaction doctrine must be met in stock-for-asset acquisitions.

From both sides of the negotiating table, the above three types of reorganization are tax free at the time of closing. Obviously, the transactions represent tax deferrals, since taxes are due and payable when stock is sold. Holders of securities in a tax-free reorganization or merger can exchange them without creating an immediate tax liability. Neither gains nor losses are recognized in such sanctioned deals.

Taxable Acquisitions

Any takeover that does not qualify as an "A", "B" or "C" type exchange would ordinarily be a taxable transaction. Thus, a company exchanging its bonds, debentures, warrants or cash, or any package of these items for the controlling stock or assets of another company would not qualify its deal as a "B" or "C" type merger, since the use of voting stock is an absolute requirement.

The big difference between a taxable merger and a tax-free merger is that in the taxable deal, an equity interest is exchanged for some non-equity interest. This difference makes the taxable deal equivalent to any other sale of securities. However, an obscure tax rule long had permitted casual sellers of property to defer their capital gains on transactions if payments received in the year of sale did not exceed 30 percent of the sale price. Payments received consisted of cash, debt securities, warrants or other property. Before the Tax Reform Act of 1969, signed into law by President Richard Nixon on December 30, 1969, bonds having serial maturities were generally not considered as payments received in the year of sale. Instead, they were considered as installment payments as they matured, or as a lump sum payment if sold prior to maturity.

By such action, it was possible to defer much of the tax on taxable exchange offers where bonds, warrants and cash were received in exchange for stock.

Through a combination of tax provisions, it had been possible before 1969, in the 1967-68 heyday of mergers, to delay tax liability and to create new tax deductions that even enabled some clever managements to structure deals that enabled them to buy companies with tax savings.

This byplay with taxable merger procedures involved three basic concepts: substituting stock for bonds, frequently with warrants; creating an installment sale; and utilizing original issue discount.

In previous years, there was a clear distinction between stocks and bonds. The investor held either an equity in the company or corporate indebtedness. For example, in the 1960's it became possible in some of the conglomerate mergers to change a stock selling at $100 and paying a $7 annual dividend into an almost equivalent position consisting of a $100, 7 percent bond with a long-term warrant to buy one share of stock at $100. Assuming the bond is usable at par to exercise the warrant, the package is theoretically equivalent to one share of stock because of its exchange value. The bond-with-warrant package is also similar to a $100 convertible bond, convertible into one share of stock, which is also a stock equivalent.

Getting back to fundamentals, there is a difference between one share of stock with voting rights and a bond-warrant package of equivalent value which does not have voting rights.

From the viewpoint of the issuing corporation, the tax advantages of issuing debt versus equity were unmistakable. If a corporation in the 50 percent tax bracket paid a $6 dividend on its common stock, it had to earn $12 a share, pre tax. Since bond interest was tax deductible, the corporation needed only to earn $6 pre tax to meet its interest obligation.

Ramifications of the 1969 Tax Reform Act

The new tax law of 1969 dealt a fatal blow to these methods of making so-called taxable mergers as attractive to investors as tax-free mergers. It also dealt a fatal blow to bonds that sold at large discounts from par, which was another twist to the tax loss position of the Federal government. When bonds were issued with warrants, it was common practice to make the bond coupon a few points below what it would have been without the warrants. When the warrants were detached from the bond, the bond tended to sell at a severe discount from par. The discount was a form of additional interest paid to the investor over the coupon rate that the issuing corporation was willing to pay at maturity rather than currently.

The issuing corporation accrued this extra interest expense and charged it off against current income. That way it got a tax deduction based on interest rates in the range of 10 to 12 percent.

The investor, however, usually reported income on a cash basis and paid tax currently on the 6 percent interest received. He deferred the original issue discount on the bond until some time in the future when the bond was redeemed or sold.

Ground Rules for Takeover

The Tax Reform Act of 1969 revised the ground rules in three areas involving corporate takeovers: (1) debt-financed corporate acquisitions, (2) installment method of taxing gains, and (3) original issue discount.

The Act specifically limits the amount of interest a corporation is allowed to deduct from its income where bonds are issued after Oct. 9, 1969 in corporate takeovers. If the corporation cannot deduct bond interest for tax purposes, the government is in effect treating the bond interest as dividends on stock. Essentially, it is closing the loophole by reversing the equity to debt conversion in takeovers.

Bonds whose interest payments come under the new restrictions must have the following characteristics: (a) the debt must be subordinated, (b) the bonds must be convertible into stock or come with warrants, and (c) the ratio of debt-to-equity must exceed 2-to-1, or average earnings for the previous three-year period must be less than three times the annual interest cost.

If the bonds meet all three characteristics, then they are considered like stock and the maximum amount of interest that can be deducted in any year for corporate tax purposes is limited to $5 million or a lesser amount in certain instances. That all but ends the bond-warrant gimmick.

While this provision will block most large mergers in which bonds and warrants are utilized, it appears that smaller takeovers may still be able to squeak through, if the aggregate interest cost falls below the $5 million mark.

After May 27, 1969, any investor who receives marketable bonds in an exchange offer for his stock will be unable to elect the installment method of reporting the profit because the value of bonds will be considered as a payment in the year of sale. Deferment of tax will be virtually impossible in the pseudo-taxable merger. Stockholders will have to think twice before they approve a bond-for-stock merger, since a large chunk of cash may be required to meet their tax cost of the exchange.

How the New Law Affects Bond Offerings

Under the new tax law, bonds issued after May 27, 1969 at a discount will carry heavier tax costs. The investor will be required to pay tax currently on a ratable portion of the original issue discount each year that he holds the bond. This attempts to match the taxable income of the bondholder with the tax deduction for bond interest and discount amortization of the issuing company.

This new rule can cause bondholders some very harsh results. For example, an investor in the 50 percent tax bracket who receives $60 bond interest and who must also pay tax on $25 of bond discount which he will only receive 30 years later—if the issuer is still in business—will nevertheless be required to pay a current tax equivalent to 71 percent of the cash received. This should make discount bonds issued in the future very unpopular.

The Tax Reform Act of 1969 did prevent gimmick mergers. However, more conventional merger activity should suffer little from this new detour on the merger road.

The Case of Bangor Punta

An example of the taxable transaction for acquisition is the May 8, 1969 agreement of Bangor Punta when it acquired just over 50 percent of the Piper Aircraft Corporation. To the common stockholders of Piper, Bangor Punta offered 1.2 common shares of its stock, warrants to purchase 3.5 common shares, and $31 principal amount of debentures. The debentures bearing interest from July 1, 1969 are initially redeemable on and after July 1, 1973 at 108.25 percent of principal amount (discount bonds), and are entitled to a sinking fund commencing on March 31, 1980 sufficient to retire by maturity 91 percent of the principal amount outstanding on March 31, 1980. The debentures are subordinate to senior indebtedness of the corporation.

The Piper family were given a different offer by Bangor Punta. For each share of their corporate stock they received one share of Bangor Punta stock, $15 principal amount of debentures, and warrants to purchase 2.2 shares of Bangor stock at $55 per share. The agreement provided that in the event Bangor Punta obtained more than 50 percent of the outstanding common stock of Piper, the Piper shareholders would thereto receive additional Bangor Punta securities and/or cash. Presumably, the Piper family shareholders should get the same total package as other Piper shareholders, since Bangor Punta did obtain more than 50 percent of the Piper stock. The matter is in the courts and the Piper family members have a taxable transaction with its liabilities to the federal government. In the market decline of 1970, the Bangor Punta package decreased sharply.

The methods of acquiring companies require a great deal of study and good tax advice. For this reason, it is well to outline the different approaches mentioned in the foregoing text.

Checklist on Acquisitions and Mergers

"Tax-Free" Reorganizations

"A" Reorganization—statutory mergers and consolidations.
  In accordance with state laws.

"B" Reorganization—stock for stock.
  Exchange must be solely for voting stock.

Acquiring corporation must have control of the acquired company after acquisition.

Earn-outs, and method payment in voting stock.

Three judicially imposed tests for the transaction:

(1) Business purpose

(2) Continuity of interest

(3) Not a step transaction.

"C" Reorganization—stock for assets.

Must acquire 90 percent of the fair market value of the net assets.

Must meet the same three judicial tests for the transaction as in the stock-for-stock acquisition.

Taxable Acquisitions

All cash or cash-installment purchases.

Installment payments may be made and subject to capital gains taxes when made if no more than 30 percent is paid in the first tax year.

Combination methods of payment.

Bonds, debentures, debentures with warrants, stock and cash may be used separately or in combination for the acquisition of a corporation in a taxable transaction. The Tax Reform Act of 1969 rules out most of the methods used in prior years, which made so-called taxable exchanges which yielded very little immediate tax returns for the government, and in some cases promised a net loss in tax revenue.

Whatever the method used for acquiring a company, it is wise to see how the structured deal may affect the buyer and the seller. The ancient adage is that the deal should be good for both sides, or there is no deal.

Buyers sometimes prefer a taxable deal since they get a "step-up" in basis. Suppose the book value of the company is $2 million and the sale price is $5 million. In a taxable transaction, the buyer is allowed to write up the assets by the amount of the gain or the sale. The buyer hopes to get a portion of the purchase price back through reduced income taxes.

Overcoming the Seller's Hurdles

The seller also has a major problem if he sells assets in a taxable deal, for he will be subject to investment credit and depreciation recapture going back to January 1, 1962. On the $3 million gain on the sale, the seller may have taken investment credits and depreciation since 1961 of $1 million. That amount would be taxable at the ordinary income rate and the balance of $2 million at the capital gains rate.

These are the kinds of problems that should be considered beforehand by both parties. In many cases, after going through the options, the buyer's offer of a stock exchange will be accepted by the seller. If the stock is listed on the market and appreciates rapidly, the seller will be happy. If the stock price declines, he will be disconsolate. However, the seller has the consolation that if market prices have declined, the selling price of his company would have been less. One other caution for the seller: the IRS applies the continuity-of-interest rule, which restricts sale of the stock to 50 percent immediately.

Knowing the variety of methods of payment available for an acquisition will greatly strengthen the bargaining position of the buyer and his ability to close the deal.

Aside from preparations for the method of purchasing another company, consideration should be given to the strategy of the meeting with the sellers. Usually the buyer likes to set the time and place of meeting. Some prefer to have the meeting at their own headquarters, or they may select a neutral ground if secrecy is important. As a general rule, it is good policy to keep the participants to no more than three persons each from the buying and selling sides; any more tend to complicate the negotiations. Many purchasers do not want legal, tax or accounting people present for the session, since they might bring up details which would kill the deal. There will be plenty of opportunity for the services of the latter group once the "gentlemen's agreement" is consummated by the principals.

Setting the Price

The most often asked question about mergers and acquisitions is: "How did the negotiators arrive at a price?" The methods of arriving at a price are as old as trade itself and as varied as the people who do the negotiating. In one example, a company put up for sale by two brothers had annual sales of some $3 million, but earnings of only 5 percent on sales, or $150,000. Even with a reappraisal of the equipment, utilizing original cost figures and granting credit wherever possible, there was no way that the net worth of the company could be brought any higher than $750,000. The brothers thought of the company as their "baby" and were oblivious to its weaknesses. They visualized their earnings not as $150,000, but by various methods of reconstitution and projection saw them as $300,000. They were generous enough to suggest that the company was for sale for ten times the reconstructed earnings, or $3 million. A little quick arithmetic will show that for an investment of $3 million, either in cash or stock, the acquiring company could depend on only $150,000 annual return, or a 20-year payout for their investment, assuming no growth.

Establishing Value

This brings up the question of rules of thumb for fixing the price of acquisitions.

From conversations with numerous executives who deal regularly in acquisitions, it is apparent that a price of 10 to 15 times earnings and hopefully not more than 150 percent of net worth is usually realistic. This normally gives two different figures and the hoped-for price would be somewhere in between. (See the discussion of evaluation procedures in the previous chapter.) However, this rule of thumb is subject to many variables since a company that has a high volume and a low net worth may be an engineering or other service business where the investment per employee is much lower than in heavy industry.

Another method of arriving at price is that utilized in the example at the end of Chapter 5. Greater American Corporation offered to pay in dollars an amount equal to the selling company's assets as reappraised to take into account equipment and other fixed assets at their current value. Added to that figure was the promise of a contingency, or deferred, payment to reflect the firm's future earnings. This has the advantage of keeping the former owners interested in the future of the business. Otherwise, they might take their hard-earned cash, continue to manage the company in a peripatetic way, and go off fishing, golfing, and traveling, which they may have been dreaming about for years.

In negotiations for acquisitions there seems to be no happy medium. Some owners have an inflated value of their company, justified, perhaps, by the blood, sweat, and tears they have put into it over a long period of time. Others who are concerned about a lack of capital, competition, the onset of new competitive products, or the need for new equipment will tend to under-value their companies. Both types usually are selling a company for the first time and would be wise to bring in an adviser in whom they have confidence and who has experience in negotiating the sale of companies. Preferably the adviser would not be solely in the legal or accounting fields, but would be conversant with the human values and human relations involved. He should also be aware of developments in the merger and acquisition world and prices currently being paid.

Another problem may arise: The seller probably has kept a record of sales of companies in his particular industry and has noted that recent sales have been at 10 to 20 times earnings. He will tend to be guided by these figures even though, under close analysis, his company, either because of its earnings potential or its possibilities for the future, warrants a higher or lower multiple.

Financial Engineering

Financial engineering is the term used to describe creative imagination when it is applied to the complex and exciting business of merger and acquisition. Unfortunately, there is a tendency to approach many deals in a meat-and-potatoes manner because the ordinary acquisition-minded individual thinks only in terms of payment by convertible -preferred stock or straight cash. The real entrepreneur and professional in the field, however, is immediately challenged by the opportunity to consider the half-dozen or more alternatives which might be utilized to gain leverage. The more he can buy with the least amount of "paper," the greater his leverage. The requisite, of course, is that any sale must be mutually advantageous, otherwise the former owners might take umbrage and attempt to cause the acquiring company to lose out in the long run. The most interesting examples of financial engineering usually involve tax problems, the seller's and buyer's, and the greatest possible use of the market place to help increase the value of the stock.

A number of the moves by James Ling and the Ling-Temco-Vought Corporation have been cited as outstanding examples of the use of the market place and the cash value of the acquired company to develop more cash to accomplish more acquisitions. When LTV purchased Wilson Packing Corporation, the first move was to spin off several parts of Wilson as subsidiaries. Next there were secondary offerings of a portion of the stock on the market. This established a value for the stock held by the parent company and at the same time brought in a bundle of cash which LTV used for additional acquisitions. However, by 1970 Ling's success faltered in the bear market because his stock collateral for loans depreciated substantially.

Financial engineering, then, is putting together the most creative deal of mutual benefit to both parties with a minimum use of cash, and the greatest use of leverage.

In one example, a company owned by two partners was purchased for 60 percent down, with the remainder of the purchase price tied to earnings over the next five years. The partners were given employment contracts for that five-year period, which served to make them responsible for earning the payout of the balance of the purchase price.

Some of the most imaginative examples of financial engineering have involved three companies rather than two. One can appreciate the complexities involved in getting three different groups to agree, the patience required to negotiate the deal, and the imagination needed to select the best method of paying for the acquisition. These three-way deals are left to the most experienced professionals in the acquisition ranks.

Understanding Contingency Payment

In earlier examples, reference was made to contingency payments tied to earnings over a stated period of time. To recapitulate, consider the purchase of a company with sales of $5 million with earnings of $350,000 after taxes, and a net worth of $2 million cash. Consider also that the former owners are to receive contingency payments over a five-year period amounting to an additional $1 million, which was tied to the company's projected earnings for that period. [It is best to permit the seller to set his own projections, since presumably he will be responsible for operating the company, and since he is best qualified to speculate on the future.] If the acquired company's projection calls for an increase in earnings of $50,000 a year from a base of $400,000, the extra $1 million might be made up by paying out 25 percent of annual pre-tax earnings after the company has earned $200,000. Therefore, if during the first year the purchased company earns $400,000 after taxes and $800,000 pre-tax, the former owners would earn the $200,000 programmed under the contingency agreement. In many contingency agreements, a safeguard is provided for the seller by stating that if the contingency is not earned in one year, there can be a carry-forward or carry-back for one or two years. The purpose is to avoid punishing the former owners for a very bad year in earnings, followed by an outstanding year.

If the company above earned only $200,000 after taxes the first year of operation under new ownership, there would be no contingency payout. However, if the next year's earnings jumped to $600,000 after taxes and $1,200,000 pre-tax, the corresponding payout would put the former owners on schedule in the contingency payments program.

In an article in the magazine *Mergers & Acquisitions*[1] in 1967, Clarence J. Hecht stated that in order to utilize contingency payments, or earn-out payments as he called them, some combination of the following conditions normally are present: (1) the acquired business must be capable of being operated as an autonomous unit; (2) the parent must be willing to leave profit and loss responsibility in the hands of the former owners; (3) the sellers must be willing through continued employment to participate in the future growth of the company that has acquired their firm.

Other writers have noted that one disadvantage of the contingency payment, or earn-out, is that if the acquiring company buys another, similar company, perhaps with a like product line, the contingency agreement becomes more difficult to fulfill because of the net effect of divided income. However, like all other challenges in business, this one is not insurmountable and some rearrangement usually can be made with the owners of the company acquired initially.

The Art of Negotiation Strategy

Negotiating the deal can be difficult and challenging. Assume that the buyer and the seller have prepared themselves adequately for the confrontation and that it has gone reasonably well. The principals on both sides have conducted themselves properly, have been reasonable in listening to alternative proposals, and have arrived at a basis for agreement. Each side has figured out what they would most like in a transaction and

[1] *Mergers & Acquisitions, The Journal of Corporate Venture.* ©1967 Mergers & Acquisitions, Inc.

both sides have come to an acceptable compromise. Students of the art of negotiation would be rife with analysis of what had taken place. Some would talk of rationalization; others would talk of motivations of love, esteem and security. Still others would stress the importance of the questions asked and the good listeners who provided favorable responses.

Still others schooled in the art of negotiation would emphasize the "when" in the strategy, saying that one side knew when to forbear and when to use strategy. In many experiences, however, none of the above have occurred. The man or men selling a company and the men buying the company are, in the mind of one observer, more interested in what Benjamin Franklin had to say. All men are interested in two worlds, wealth and prestige. If they are seeking wealth, one approach is required; if they have wealth and want prestige, another ploy is needed.

In dealings with an owner of a publicly owned company, prestige is more important. To the owner of a privately owned company, newly opened paths to wealth are most often the key.

In dealings with an owner of a privately owned company, the acquisition may make him an instant millionaire. Assuming that he has wealth in the nature of an equity which he cannot market, he may feel "poor" and see a whole new world of high finance available through the sale of his company. A psychologist made this interesting comment: "I don't want to predict how I would act if suddenly one day I became a wealthy man with means that I could utilize as I wished." All the more reason for the contingency payment, which requires performance for up to five years by the purchased company. One seller characterized it as the "nose to the grindstone approach" and that is a proper reaction. Moreover, from the buyer's view, he knows that the former owners of a privately owned corporation will not take advantage of him.

Most negotiations proceed at a good pace and most participants are realistic enough to see the advantages and disadvantages of a deal. Most often there is a give and take and the members are ready, within certain ranges, to make a deal, or else they would not be present.

The deal is usually negotiated within certain boundaries and certain rules of play, and many deals are negotiated within what seems to the observer to be a very casual relationship. Usually, if a deal is to be consummated, the principals know the various approaches. For example, one deal involved a company which was for sale by one owner. The owner was not interested in preferred stock and an explanation of what this would mean in the future. At the same time, another company was besieging the owner with telephone calls, seeking to frustrate the sale. An approach which might be called the "soft sell" was successful. There was no attempt to pressure the deal or to take away what rightfully belonged to the owner. The settlement was a straight cash deal and for only a few dollars more than what the other group offered.

Cases in Point

In another negotiation, the two youthful owners of a growing company were considering several offers. They were growing fast and needed working capital. On the day of decision they were bedevilled with tax problems, all personal in nature. They wanted a takeover candidate who would solve their tax problems and give the company the financial stability it needed.

Two owners of another company were doing well for the first time in ten years. They were not old, but they were worried about what might happen if one of them was suddenly taken out of the picture by death. They gladly sold their company for a down payment, plus contingency payments based on earnings, and employment contracts for the six-year life of the contingency payments.

Another company was owned by three men, all employees who had helped build the company. The untimely death of the owner-manager handed them the company as long as they paid the estate. To do so took every bit of their capital and credit. They needed a partner, someone who would take over, relieve them of their debt load, and have a stake in the business they were willing to help build.

These are some of the reasons men sell their companies, and also some of the reasons why negotiations succeed or fail. The buyer must know the circumstances and how to play them without going too far or too fast. Negotiations are a complex matter and a challenge, and many circumstances and conditions must be taken into account without overdoing the proposal.

What Kills the Deal

In negotiations, price and the method of payment, the tender offers, and the different methods of handling negotiations are of extreme importance. Often, however, the key is not the money involved, but whether there is empathy between the buyer and the seller. The owners of smaller companies, or their professional managers, may, in the course of negotiations, become frightened by the acquisitive nature, and even somewhat domineering attitude, of the people with whom they are dealing. Perhaps they are concerned because some word of the negotiations has leaked out, with the result that two or three of their most valued executives have expressed a desire to leave. There are a great many reasons why a deal can go wrong. The very fine journal of corporate venture, *Mergers & Acquisitions,* in an article in the March-April 1968 issue by Senior Editor Joseph S. D'Aleo concluded that it is not just luck or a favorable stock market, but many other factors which make the deal come to completion. Mr.

D'Aleo checked several hundred terminations during the 1967 and early 1968 period and found that a number of conclusions could be drawn as to why deals had failed. He stated that: (1) About half of the deals should not have been allowed to reach the board of directors for a vote because there was a clash of management, or the product mix was too great a problem. (2) Wild gyrations in the price of stock of one of the would-be partners, or opposing price movements on the market in the company's share, could render a deal impossible. (3) Negotiations can cool quickly if there is a threat of an anti-trust suit, or if there are difficult legal snarls, strikes or threats of legal action from shareholders. One exception D'Aleo noted was the proposed International Telephone and Telegraph/American Broadcasting Corporation merger in which ITT hung on to ABC for nearly two years before giving it up. It is interesting to note that ABC subsequently went through a shorter, but no less difficult, courtship by Howard Hughes, which also ended in failure. (4) Family-owned businesses can be troublesome because one or more of the members of the family may suddenly decide to change his mind.

The Central Causes of Failure

D'Aleo discussed the reasons for the terminations he studied and what took place, the names of the partners, and the lengths of the talks. The most common reasons for termination were the threat of anti-trust action and the weakness or drop off in the purchase of stock. The latter reason is presumably good evidence that the stock was selling at a very high price earnings ratio and a drop off prevented the would-be buyer from offering the rather high premium called for in the deal. Becton Dickinson dealt with Univis for three months and finally gave up because of legal suits. Utah Construction in its takeover attempt of Bunker Hill Company over a four-month period finally saw the breakdown of negotiations because the market price of the stock dropped off. The same reason was given for the short courtship of Allis-Chalmers by Signal Oil and Gas. In the case of the negotiations between Kansas-Nebraska Natural Gas and United Utilities, which extended over five months, regulatory problems as well as legal snarls made fulfillment impossible. A clash of management occurred between the M-G-M and Teleprompter groups during a seven-month negotiating period. It is conceivable that extended negotiations suffer some of the strains of long human engagements. Only one breakdown of merger negotiations of the group cited by D'Aleo was occasioned by tax status problems, and that was the proposed deal between Gamble-Skogmo and the Red Owl stores.

There is also the actual experience of the seller, who, representing 100 percent of the stock of a company, walked into a meeting with prospective purchasers and said, "I will take $2 million for my company. If you want to offer less forget it!" This "take-it-or-leave-it" attitude can kill almost any deal, unless the acquiring company has the patience and a strong desire to buy the company. This approach naturally raises the question as to whether the purchaser would want to retain the former owner as the chief executive. Incidentally, in the above case, the asking price of $2 million was double the net worth of the company and a prohibitive figure since the company had not had the kind of growth that would warrant such a payment.

Chapter 7

HOW TO WAGE THE BATTLE OF TENDERS AND COMPETING OFFERS

In mergers and acquisitions, the majority of deals are negotiated person-to-person by the top management or owners of publicly and privately held companies. Cash, stock or notes, or some combination is used to purchase a corporation. The negotiations are most often conducted in good faith and in a friendly spirit. When agreement is reached, the parent company and its acquisition must attempt to make the marriage work.

There is another method of acquisition which is, on some occasions, the direct antithesis of the above normal situation. Two giants square off in what is known literally as a tender battle. Only a company whose stock is listed on a major exchange is the subject of a tender offer—and this limits the battle ground to less than 4,000 corporations. The maker of the tender offer is usually another member of this elite group of America's largest corporations, but the ground rules also permit a concentration of money in private or public hands to get into the competition.

A full discussion of tender offers and the defense against them is pertinent since acquisition-minded executives may find themselves on one side or the other in a tender battle. This chapter will consider:

1. The kinds of corporations subject to tender offers.
2. Defenses possible for the company under attack.
3. How the battle of the tender is waged.
4. What happens when other corporations enter the arena with competing offers.

In the past few years, tender offers have emerged as an effective and often-used acquisition tool. They are a valid instrument for gaining working control or majority control of another corporation by paying a premium to its shareholders in a public offering.

There were in 1965 twenty-nine cash tender offers to acquire companies listed on the New York Stock Exchange and fifteen tenders for companies listed on the American Stock Exchange. Five years previously, in 1960, there were only eight tender offers to corporations listed on both exchanges. The pace has quickened so that today we are witness to a hundred or more tender offers each year.

To set the record straight, tender offers are usually made when the management of the offering company believes that the subject company will endorse the tender offer or at least not actively oppose it. The objective should be to quiet the opposition since it removes obstacles to the success of the tender offer and oftentimes means that the tender can be made at a lower price per share. However, contested tender offers do capture the imagination of the business community as the battle is waged in publications, in news stories, and in classical full-page advertisements.

What Prompts the Tender Offer

Paradoxically, a tender offer when uncontested may be less expensive than the conventional form of acquisition. The tender technique will usually permit the acquiring company to gain control by purchasing a smaller portion of the acquired company than would otherwise be necessary. The comparison of a smaller payout is valid when the alternative and conventional acquisition is a purchase of assets for cash or stock. Most successful tender offers are followed by merger, so vote control in the acquired company is the objective.

Another reason for a tender offer is that the management may be cool to a conventional acquisition move. A tender offer makes the stage public and puts the decision up to the stockholders.

Another advantage to the tender offer is that there is less possibility of judicial questioning as to the fairness of the price paid than there might be in the purchase of assets or a stock swap. In a tender offer for control or takeover, each shareholder makes his own decision, but whether or not he tenders his stock, he must realize that the majority rules if the tender offer for control is successful. Most state laws have a provision permitting an aggrieved stockholder to be paid the appraised value of his stock in the acquired company as it was prior to the successful tender offer.

The Disadvantages of the Tender Offer

The tender offer as an alternative to merger or acquisition of assets has its penalties. Obviously, the tendering corporation cannot make the kind of detailed investigation possible with the cooperation of management in the conventional purchase. The acquiring company, moreover, frequently pays more for each share purchased in the block than it would if it were buying all the shares. The increased price is a result of the necessity of offering a sizable premium.

The popularity of the tender offer technique, however, created a great deal of interest within the Securities and Exchange Commission and Congress, where particular attention was being given to certain tender offers which took the form of a "corporate raid." Further clouding the issue was the fact that some individuals or groups making tender offers did not wish to be known and hid behind "street" names, meaning the names of brokerage houses, or numbered accounts in Swiss banks. This cloak of secrecy added to the concern of the stockholders who were the target of the offer and challenged to some extent the validity of the technique.

Inevitably, the skirmishing over the uncontrolled aspects of tender offers resulted in regulation. The applicable Public Law 90-439 of July 29, 1968, requires that any person proposing to make a cash tender offer which would give him ownership of more than 10 percent of the outstanding stock of a corporation must first file a statement with the Securities and Exchange Commission.

The statement must show:

1. The number of shares he owns or has options on;
2. His background and identity;
3. The source and amount of funds to be used in making the purchases, including information as to borrowed funds;
4. Any plans he has, should he gain control, to liquidate, sell the assets of, or merge the corporation, or make any other major change in business or corporate structure; and
5. General information as to particular arrangements he may have concerning the stock (such as joint ventures, the voting of proxies, etc.).

The foregoing regulation makes a whole new ballgame of tender offers. It also underlines the magic figure of 10 percent stock ownership and explains why makers of tender offers and raiders often purchase 9.9 percent of the stock before making their tender offer.

Which Corporations Are Most Vulnerable

What kinds of corporations are the target of tender offers? *Finance Magazine* published each month a list of a half dozen corporations under the heading "Takeover Candidates." *The New York Times* in January, 1969, said: "It is part of the conventional wisdom that a company that earns little, cuts its dividend and has lots of money in its treasury is not only a good take-over possibility but also is a poorly managed company that deserves to be gobbled up."

By the natural selection of a Darwinian theory of business is it not better that the assets a company is hoarding be put to good use? Many observers think the process has gone too far in this day of widely held shareholdings, where it is rare that the professional management owns more than a few percent of the company's stock. In effect, every major company, no matter how well managed, is a sitting duck for the big game hunter. And as on safari, most of the weapons are in the hands of the hunter.

The maker of a tender offer may secretly acquire a substantial position, under 10 percent of the target company's stock, by buying from a mutual fund or large stockholder at a price which gives the shareowner a neat windfall profit. Then he can approach the company directly and use his leverage to get consent to the purchase.

If the reception is not enthusiastic, the offerer can mount a blitz attack before the management can mobilize a defense. Many of the most telling defensive moves take time and, often, the consent of the stockholders.

The take-over candidate may wonder how it all happened. Like the ostrich, it may have chosen to put its head in the sand, it may have failed to make optimum use of company assets, and its stock consequently may be selling at or near book value. The company should have been moving into promising growth areas of business, combing the field for potential acquisitions. But the latter idea runs contrary to the thinking of some managements, although the fate of such "conservative" companies makes a strong argument why all corporations should today be interested and active in merger and acquisitions.

Defense Against Takeover

What defenses are possible for the company that is a take-over candidate? The future planning organization of the company should be on constant lookout for acquisitions. Such purchases made for stock serve to dilute the position of the potential raider and most often put blocks of company stock in friendly hands. Defense-minded managements should ask the stockholders at an annual or special meeting for additional authorized stock, both common and preferred, to have available for quick acquisitions. If you suspect there are outside designs on your company, you can acquire companies for up to 18.5 percent of your outstanding stock without stockholder approval or registration with the SEC or the New York Stock Exchange.

The management has available a large number of stockholders which should be assiduously cultivated. This will require more communication with the smaller stockholders and even plant visits and special explanatory meetings with larger holders. Another advantageous move is for the president and board members to attempt to interest mutual funds and pension funds in large stock purchases because of the likelihood that these groups will become allies. However, the low return on your stock and an unattractive market price make this ploy more difficult, unless you can show that your plans for the future will result in increased earnings.

Ask any Wall Streeter for the perfect defense against a corporate take-over, and he will tell you instantly: a high price-earnings ratio. No maker of tender offers wants to buy in at 20 to 30 times earnings. The raider will probably turn to a less high-priced property.

How the Tender Offer Battle Is Waged

The most common target of a tender offer is the fairly large company with a substantial net worth which is not making a reasonable return on investment. Most of these target companies are listed on the stock exchanges and because of the great mass of statistical data available today on listed companies, they stick out like "sore thumbs." Standard Statistics has computerized data on all the major listed industrial corporations, and on all the major utility and insurance companies as well. A quick check of the stock ownership will indicate that in some of these companies there are no holdings of sizable blocks of stock of 5 percent or more, and the management owns less than 5 percent. Thus, for an undervalued stock, selling at close to its book value, a buyer can make a tender offer with a premium of 10 percent to 15 percent of the market value and expect to get 30 percent or 40 percent of the company, or the percentage needed to gain working control. The tender offer is not a difficult device to use since certain advertisements and other information presented to the SEC is all that is necessary to get the action going. A date is named, an address where the stock can be sent is indicated, and a definite price commitment is made. Most tender offers include a release clause which permits the acquiring company to cease buying after it has purchased a certain number of shares, perhaps 500,000.

Shoring Up for the Battle

The takeover group always asks for the stockholder list and newspaper accounts are full of battles over which group will get the list, and why the "victim's" management is struggling to keep the list from the attacking faction. Usually the courts will decide in favor of the request, and the target company, after a fight, reluctantly surrenders the stock list. However, this means delay and in the meantime another group may enter the bidding for the company.

Much has been written about defense against a takeover bid. It is true that the maker of the tender offer has surprise on his side, plus the lure of a premium above the market price. However, in recent situations the market has very quickly moved to the price of the tender offer, causing the premium to lose a great deal of its appeal.

Moreover, management has the resources of its treasury to defend against tender offers. Internally, the target company can defend its position with a great deal of publicity and advertising, by direct mail to the stockholders, and by utilizing its contacts with banks, insurance companies, brokers, and others to help round up stockholders who may pledge their support to the company.

There are other methods whereby management and the board of directors can fight off tender offers. One is to actively seek a desirable third party which has been subject to tender offers. A quick review of these companies may produce a more desirable partner than the one making the tender offer. Situations have arisen in which the company being sought had already been sold, or had already arranged a sale to another larger company, before the original offer could be consummated.

Some Interesting Variations

One neat ploy in the defense against raiders has been taken by several large corporations. At the annual meeting of United Nuclear Corporation, shareholders approved a charter change requiring 80 percent stockholder approval of a takeover bid. Most corporate by-laws require only a two-thirds vote in favor. Oddly enough, a year before, Combustion Engineering Inc. passed a similar amendment shortly before embarking on an attempt to win control of United Nuclear.

Specifically, the United Nuclear charter amendment says that 80 percent shareholder approval would be required for a merger with a company holding more than 10 percent of any class of United Nuclear's equity securities. Combustion Engineering held about 21 percent of the stock. United Nuclear shareholders at the same time approved an increase in authorized common shares to 10 million from the previous 7 million and created a new class of 2 million shares of series preferred stock.

One of the dangers of buying another company's shares is evident in the Combustion Engineering-United Nuclear situation. Combustion purchased United Nuclear stock when the price was high. In a falling market, the stock has dropped substantially and if Combustion Engineering must dispose of it because of a Court order, the company faces a serious financial loss.

In another example, Westinghouse Air Brake found itself in a contest with the Crane Company, which wanted to take over. WABCO's board of directors agreed in principle to merge into American Standard as a defense, but the situation got sticky. Crane had initiated the contest with a series of cash purchases of WABCO stock. When the Westinghouse Air Brake called a stockholder's meeting to approve the merger with American Standard, a legal battle to set aside the proxies ensued. Crane claimed that the proxy statement was misleading because it did not say the reason for the merger was to forestall Crane's takeover bid. The court held that because the proxy statement disclosed Crane's outstanding purchase offer, and because WABCO's present management would continue after the merger, it was not misleading. The court emphasized that the disclosure rules are concerned with facts, not motives. The court victory went to American Standard and presumably WABCO was successful in its defense.

One of the Fastest Cases on Record

One victim of a tender offer tells this story. He, the president, and his top management were pleased at renewed activity in their stock. But the financial reports and earnings prospects were not promising enough to warrant this new interest.

One morning a visitor called to say that he represented the group making the stock purchases; the group now owned almost 10 percent of the company stock. He informed the management that he controlled 300,000 of the 2,900,000 shares outstanding, which made him one of the larger stockholders.

His plans were quickly detailed. His lawyers would register with SEC a prospectus detailing an offer of $50 subordinated convertible debentures paying 6 percent interest for each share of the target company's stock. This would be convertible at any time on a share-for-share basis into the company's stock, which was currently selling at $40 per share. In addition, each debenture would carry a warrant to purchase a share of the company's stock at $55. The whole package would be offered to the company's stockholders on a one-for-one basis for 1,500,000 shares, enough to give the "raider" control.

The president could see the attractiveness of the tender offer to the stockholders who were getting only $1.75 per share in dividends. The new plan would give them an interest payment of $3 per share. To this would be added the premium for the conversion right and the anticipated value of the warrants, which would most probably have a public market.

When the visitor left, there was shocked silence and the repeated question, "Why did this happen to us?" Within an hour the visitor's press release was in the newspapers and the Dow-Jones broad tape carried it. A flood of buy orders arrived and the company stock could not be traded for an hour. When the market on the stock re-opened the price had jumped 6 points. By close of trading, 110,000 shares had been traded, twenty times the normal daily volume.

Within a week almost 1,500,000 shares, or over half the stock outstanding, had been traded. The raider, meanwhile, was counting his gains, which "Uncle Sam" would help him make. On the dividends he expected to receive from the company's stock, he would pay only a small tax, since 85 percent of dividends are excluded from taxation. Of his debenture interest of $3 per share, he would be able to write off half as an expense of doing business, making the cost only $1.50.

Most important, however, was the fact that Mr. Raider would have the benefit of having his hands on the controls of the company. He could be expected to re-constitute the board of directors in his own image, and ask the management to work up an action program for acquisitions. As a final touch, the proceeds of the warrants would go to benefit the raider's company.

The Performance Game

Quite often in recent years, two or more groups have focused their attention on the same takeover candidate. Then there is a battle royal to titillate Wall Streeters and all who follow corporate news. Thus, no discussion of merger and acquisition negotiations would be complete without a look at what some observers call the "performance game."

It seems nowadays that when a large company makes a bid to buy up the shares of another company, somebody else horns in with a rival bid. Why does this happen so often?

You do not have to probe deeply into today's securities markets to find the answer. A number of corporations with aggressive financial officers are in the "performance game" up to their necks. In the process, they have found that the competitive merger proposal is a gambit with which it is nearly impossible to lose in a bull market and with which one may easily turn a fat profit.

The most amazing such profit was variously estimated at $25 million to $30 million. It was reaped by Gulf & Western Industries, Inc., when G. & W. made an offer for shares of Sinclair Oil Company, and pressed the offer after Sinclair decided to merge with Atlantic Richfield Corporation. The price of the stock of Sinclair, a big but rather colorless oil company, rose from 80 to around 136 in the rivalry.

This was the third time in recent years that G. & W. reaped big profits by starting merger proposals or buying stakes in other companies and then selling out. G. & W. bought 3,248,000 shares of Allis-Chalmers, in what looked like an acquisition bid, at prices reported to be about $28. It then sold them at $35, profiting by many millions. G. & W. also turned over a profit of $8 million to $10 million on a big block of Pan American World Airways.

Profits from Unsuccessful Takeover Bids

Several other big profits have been made through takeover bids that did not go through. Loew's Theatres, Inc., is reported to have made $21 million by re-selling one million shares of Commercial Credit Company to Control Data Corporation.

Bangor Punta Corporation figured in two such deals, making a profit of about $700,000 in an unsuccessful contest with American Machine & Foundry Corporation over Harley Davidson Motors of Milwaukee, and reaping $375,000 by buying into Blaw-Knox, then selling out to the rival bidder, White Consolidated, Inc. Such deals may, however, be subject of suits to recover the stock price gains.

There are others; Meshulam Riklis's Rapid American Corporation made an almost overnight profit of $2 million in shares in Schenley Industries. This one had its humorous side. Another Riklis company, Glen Alden, eventually acquired control of Schenley, but Rapid American's financial management apparently could not resist the temptation to sell its Schenley stock and take the profit at about the same time.

In a litigated case, Thomas Mellon Evans' Crane Company lost its bitter fight to take over Westinghouse Air Brake Company of Pittsburgh to American Standard Inc. Crane subsequently sold on the open market for about $76 million the American Standard securities it received for its WABCO stock when the merger was consummated. Crane admitted a profit on the deal, but did not say how much. American Standard has a suit against Crane in the Federal courts seeking to recover whatever short-term profit Crane made on the stock, claiming Crane violated insider trading rules of the Securities Act of 1934.

Tender Offer Competition

Possibly the record for simultaneous tender offers is held by Atlantic Research Corporation. In 1966 no less than four suitors made tender offers for this company, whose stock was listed on the American Exchange. Ogden Corporation in a second tender offered $27 per share; Singer Company, $30; Whittaker Corporation, $33.10; and finally Susquehanna Corporation, $36. The last-named acquired Atlantic Research and has continued to be active in the tender offer business. However, it fell prey to the worst of all blows when its stock, which ran up spectacularly to over $80 per share, fell into the low teens. Its good right arm in the tender market was ailing and tender offers were not in the ball game.

Seldom has a merger bid caught as much attention as Northwest Industries' tender to buy the prestigious B.F. Goodrich Company in 1969. It is an excellent case study. Ben W. Heineman, President of Northwest, tenaciously pursued Goodrich, whose Chairman, J. Ward Keener, resisted with desperation and ingenuity. As *Business Week* said, "Partly because the law binds Northwest officials to silence while their tender offer is in effect, the ball has remained in Goodrich's corner, and it has been used with telling effect."

Goodrich took out full-page ads in newspapers around the country telling its stockholders of "Ten Dangers in Tendering Even One Share to Northwest Industries." Northwest had to report a 50 percent drop in second-quarter earnings and its stock slid to 15-5/8, down from a 1969 high of 46.

Also, Goodrich filed a federal suit asking that the Northwest offer be blocked until the Interstate Commerce Commission approved the deal. Goodrich contended that ICC approval was needed because the routes of Northwest's Chicago & Northwestern Railroad were near those of Motor Freight Corporation, a trucking company which Goodrich had bought after Northwest began its takeover effort.

Weighing the Human Costs

The candidate for a takeover should not overlook a very common defense—the matter of complaining to the Justice Department or the Federal Trade Commission that the acquisition would violate the anti-trust laws. In fact, some of the government's most successful anti-trust cases have resulted from this sort of situation, since the government is much more likely to win when there is a ready source of damaging evidence.

Tender offers are usually presented from a financial side, leaving out of consideration the frightful costs in human values. During a tender offer, the great bulk of employees are fearful of their jobs, unsure of the future. It is certain that whether the tender is made or whether it is fought off, life in the company will never be the same. The subsequent merger after a successful tender offer is bound to change the long-held prospects for advancement by many executives, though it usually does not have as great an effect upon the rank-and-file employees. Morale is an important problem in all mergers and acquisitions and will be treated in Chapter 10, the post-merger situation. For those wishing to arm themselves against tender offers, Arthur Schmidt & Associates has available a "Checklist for Anticipating and Fighting A Tender Offer." In outline form it tells the danger signs, early warning signals and detection methods, preparations for defense, and the various strategies to be used.

Chapter 8

TAKING GOVERNMENTAL CONSIDERATIONS INTO ACCOUNT

When the buyer and seller have reached an understanding about a proposed acquisition, they should consider what effect the transaction may have on other interested parties. For example, our federal government and our society demand that the buyer and seller consider the public, the creditors of the seller (and sometimes of the buyer), and the stockholders of both, all of whom have a vested interest in the transaction.

Legal and Financial Implications

The public's interest in any acquisition or merger is both financial and legal. The laws are very explicit in establishing safeguards against monopoly and unreasonable restraints of trade, and the laws regulating the sales of securities are designed to protect the public interest, as well as the stockholders of both the buyer and seller as part owners of the business. The determination of the nature and effect of the rights of the public, creditors, and stockholders is a legal problem and at this point in the negotiations the lawyers for the buyer and seller, if they have not already taken part, should certainly be consulted. They should first be instructed to put together a binding memorandum covering the points both parties have agreed to thus far. Next, before a contract is developed, the lawyers should consider what problems, if any, will be created by tax restrictions, antitrust laws, Securities Exchange Commission (SEC) and other regulatory commission requirements, state "Blue-Sky" laws, and stock exchange requirements. It should be noted that out of the total of 3,000 acquisitions in 1967, 100 were singled out for antitrust action. Currently, complaints for alleged breach of Section 7 of the Clayton Act, which prohibits acquisitions that may lessen competition, are running at some 26 a year. Moreover, the impact of rules and regulations on the merger market is felt most in horizontal mergers, where a company seeks to make acquisitions in its own field.

Legal Restrictions

Restrictions placed on a company by the federal government as a result of an antitrust litigation can have a serious effect for years. In 1968, for example, the management of Procter & Gamble Company agreed that for seven years it would not, without the approval of the Federal Trade Commission (FTC) acquire any company worth more than $25,000 engaged in the manufacture, production, sale or distribution of consumer products. The company also agreed that for 10 years it would not, without FTC approval, acquire any organization engaged in growing, producing, importing, manufacturing, or processing coffee or coffee products in the United States. This restrictive ruling preventing Procter & Gamble from expanding its markets resulted from an FTC challenge of P & G's 1963 acquisition of coffee processor, J.A. Folger & Company.

National Cleaning Contractors, Inc., of New York, similarly agreed that it would not acquire any interest in any general cleaning and maintenance contractor in the metropolitan area. The Justice Department also placed a further five-year restriction on the company requiring it to give prior approval before making an acquisition.

On the other hand, such government challenges, coming at times long after the fact, often result in the spinning off, or sale, of divisions and companies which are gobbled up by other acquisition-minded companies. In 1969, for example, General Foods sold its SOS soap pad business, bought from the Purex Corporation in 1956, to Miles Laboratories for $56 million cash. The sale followed a lengthy court battle against an FTC divestiture order requiring General Foods to sell SOS. Management must allow for the possibility that it will be forced to sell off an acquisition years down the road. The question then arises whether it will be a distress sale or whether the acquired company will make a profit during the years the divestiture is being contested. If the latter situation occurs, the sale can be made at a good profit.

The list of recent divestitures includes many "Blue Chip" names. Monsanto consented to dispose of Mobay Chemical Company; Rexall Drug & Chemical Company gave up Imco Container Company; and General Motors Corporation disposed of its Euclid Division, a major truck builder.

These actions involved acquisitions of firms in fields in which the divesting company already had major interests. The caution implicit in these government orders is that merger-minded personnel must think twice before considering the acquisition of a company in their line of endeavor. Paradoxically, this government attitude causes executives to look into fields other than their own for acquisitions, and thus spawns the conglomerate trend.

The Case of the Maremont Corporation

One of the FTC's most far reaching challenges has been levelled against the Maremont Corporation. The action covers 40 properties acquired since 1953, primarily in the auto parts rebuilding industry. The FTC action was no surprise to the industry since Maremont had been consistently buying warehouse distributors. The FTC charge is that Maremont has shut the door to products of competitors and that the company now holds a "decisive competitive advantage."

Clearly, government regulatory agencies, through the operation of administrative law, have much to say about mergers and acquisitions. This is not to suggest that the acquiring executive attempt to make himself knowledgeable in this field, but it is to stress that in negotiating acquisitions he would be prudent to have legal counsel available. As a practical matter, it is unlikely that the acquiring executive will run into government regulation from other than the SEC and the Internal Revenue Service (IRS), unless his endeavors are in radio and television, which is the domain of the Federal Communications Commission (FCC), or in transportation where the Interstate Commerce Commission (ICC) and the Civil Aeronautics Board (CAB) reign. In the general area of horizontal acquisitions considered in restraint of trade, his actions will come under the Federal Trade Commission, previously mentioned in the case of Procter & Gamble. Also, if the acquisition interests are in banking, expect that the Comptroller of the Currency, and possibly the Federal Reserve Commission (FRC), may have much to say about the expansion desires. The hand of the federal government is not in every contemplated transaction, in fact it is in very few, but as one interested in acquisitions you should discuss merger interests with your counsel before getting into areas of government interest.

Securities and Exchange Commission Requirements

Certain provisions of the law and certain regulations have a direct bearing on acquisitions. Since the Securities Act of 1933 concerns itself, however, only with the sale of securities, it poses no problem in the acquisition of a going business if the buyer uses cash. If, on the other hand, the buyer purchases the stock of the seller for cash with a view to distributing the stock, or if subsequently he proposes to dispose of the stock, the buyer must take into account the provisions of the Act and the regulations of the SEC.

The Securities Act of 1933 contains an all-inclusive provision stating that unless a registration statement is in effect with the SEC, it is unlawful for any person to use any means of interstate commerce to sell any security. In general, the use of stock or securities by a buyer to acquire a company is considered a sale by the Act. Accordingly, the buyer, if he uses stock to acquire a company without a registration statement being effective, must realize that he is in violation of the Securities Act of 1933, unless he has in hand an exemption for the transaction. Fortunately, not all the sales of securities require the filing of a registration statement. Under the specific provisions of the Securities Act of 1933, state, municipal, and federal securities are exempt, as is the issuance of securities to persons resident within a single state or territory, and the issuance of securities by a corporation not involving any public offering.

The SEC as a Watchdog

As a rough rule of thumb, acquisition-minded executives had best figure that any of their actions will require consideration by the SEC. For example, SEC rules require conglomerates, as of August 14, 1969, to reveal the contribution to sales and before-tax earnings of all major lines of business. You can be sure that this restricts the conglomerates, but it also opens up a whole new line of inquiry and search by those looking for acquisitions. The expectation is that conglomerates with divisions and subsidiaries that are not carrying their weight may be looking for opportunities to sell off these non-profitable interests.

Many corporate executives fear that fuller disclosure as required by SEC could lead to all sorts of problems; competitors, for example, might get useful information. And investors might try to force the sale of unprofitable divisions.

Already, a growing number of companies are divesting themselves of their less profitable, or misfit, acquisitions. For the most part, the disposition of out-and-out losers is the most common reason for selling an acquired company, but there are other reasons. For one, acquisition-minded companies are becoming a great deal more sophisticated in balancing their businesses. For another, acquiring companies appear more anxious to sell off smaller lines or businesses that came along as part of a larger deal.

How Some Corporations Fared with the SEC

USM Corporation of Boston sold Inpack Systems Divisions, purchased in 1964, because the plastic packaging equipment maker did not meet expectations; its leasing operations just did not generate enough cash flow to suit USM.

Standard International Corporation sold its household products division, but had to do so in pieces. Supporting the thesis that it is often more difficult to sell well than to buy well, Standard could not find a suitable buyer for the entire division. Result: Standard sold Lestoil to Noxell Corporation and Bon Ami to Sterling Drugs, Inc.

Some corporate strategists call it redirection of capital resources and one of the leading practitioners of this technique has been James Ling whose Ling-Temco-Vought, Inc. decided to sell all or parts of Computer Technology, Inc., Braniff Airways, Inc., and Whitehall Electronics Corporation.

The heart of the SEC disclosure rule requires companies with sales of more than $50 million a year to report separately on those products or services that contribute at least 10 percent to total sales and operating revenue. The requirement was eased to 15 percent for smaller companies.

The new regulation also requires separate disclosure of any product line that results in a loss equal to at least 10 percent of the gross income of larger companies and 15 percent of smaller firms. It further provides that when a company has more than 10 lines of business, disclosure may be limited to the "10 most important lines."

In addition, the acquiring executive should be aware that the SEC requirements are concerned not only with registration and reporting but also with limitations on disposition of securities. Wolfson ran afoul of some of these regulations dealing with unregistered stock.

The SEC has powers to challenge acquisitions that come under its regulations dealing with insider transactions. There are also requirements for FTC and Justice Department pre-acquisition clearance that one should be aware of.

Federal Trade Commission

This agency is responsible, along with the Justice Department, for anti-trust action. By mid-1968, the Commission had computerized the merger movement and produced a profile of corporate activity. In the same year, the FTC decreed that companies planning to merge must let 60 days elapse between the notification to the government and the consummation of the merger. When the New York City Bar Association complained that the 60-day waiting period would amount to "an automatic preliminary injunction," the agency backed down somewhat stating that the waiting period and notification was operative "only when the particular merger schedule permitted."

Meanwhile, the FTC, through the use of its computer, is keeping a close watch on acquisitions. It has noted that the first purchase of a company with more than $100 million in assets was Olin Mathieson Chemical Corporation's acquisition of E.R. Squibb & Sons. In the following 10 years, there were only three or four equally huge purchases each year. Then the movement took off. From five mergers exceeding $100 million in 1963, the pace jumped to 23 in 1967, and a half dozen of those mergers exceeded $250 million.

Antitrust Problems

James J. Ling, the former merger king, in a speech at Fort Worth, Texas in July

1968 had this reaction to government "interference": "I mentioned a while back the problem of harassment from Washington. Frankly, I have a feeling that some of the people in the Justice Department confuse Rome with Washington. I personally do not believe that they are completely infallible in matters such as mergers, acquisitions, conglomerates, etc., etc., ad nauseum. As some of you know, we have tangled with them on a few occasions. The first time was when Ling-Temco, a small metal bending sub-contracting electronics firm, acquired Chance Vought. The Justice Department rushed in with an anti-trust suit, charging that the then new LTV, without any question or doubt, even though we were not in the commercial airplane business and did not have a single new contract on the books, would, as a result of this merger, put Boeing, Douglas, General Dynamics, Lockheed, etc., out of business. Now this notorious, unwarranted attack on LTV cost us dearly in time and dollars in a period when we could little afford either."

Ling had hardly warmed up. He continued: "The second time we tangled with the Justice Department was two years ago concerning Okonite. Again, the Justice Department rushed in, but this time they hedged their bet. First they said that LTV would probably, as the owners of Okonite, make it unbearably competitive for the other large wire and cable manufacturing companies including Westinghouse, General Electric, General Wire and Cable, and others.Then they suggested that if this were not to happen we probably would not be good managers and as a result Okonite might go out of business. They attacked us on both sides: we were overly competitive or completely incompetent."

The Justice Department issued a 27-page set of "merger guidelines" in May, 1968 that in their immediate effect changed nothing, but they did shed much light on Justice Department enforcement interests. The guidelines state specifically that the government will continue to challenge these three types of mergers:

1. The so-called "horizontal" mergers involving direct competitors where in highly concentrated markets the acquiring company and the acquired company each account for as little as 4 percent of their market.

2. "Vertical" mergers involving suppliers and their customers, such as a shoe manufacturer and a shoe retailer, where the supplier accounts for 10 percent or more of total market sales and the customer accounts for 6 percent or more of total market purchases.

3. "Conglomerate" mergers, defined as those that are neither horizontal or vertical, where a very large company that might have entered a new business through internal expansion enters instead by acquiring an important concern already in the business; where the merger creates dangers of reciprocal buying; and where the acquiring company's promotional resources are so great as to enhance an acquired company's existing dominance in the field.

Three antitrust problems must be considered in any acquisition: 1) whether the buyer will inherit liability for any past violations of antitrust laws on the part of the seller; 2) whether the acquisition in and of itself constitutes a violation of the antitrust laws; and 3) whether the intended future conduct of the business by the buyer may result in any violations of the antitrust laws.

A complete discussion of antitrust laws is far beyond the scope of this volume for many books have been written about individual statutes which constitute this segment of corporate law. There are four different federal laws that affect acquisitions. The first is Section 7 of the Clayton Act, which addresses itself specifically to acquisitions. Section 7 of the Clayton Act provides that the Act is violated when a corporation acquires assets or stock in another corporation and the effect of the acquisition may be substantially to lessen competition or to tend to create a monopoly.

Implications of the Key Legislation

The second act which must be read together with the Clayton Act is the Sherman Act. This provides that "every contract, combination in the form of trust or otherwise, or conspiracy, in restraint of trade or commerce . . . is declared to be illegal." Further, it states that "every person who shall monopolize, or attempt to monopolize, or . . . conspire . . . to monopolize any part of . . . . commerce" shall violate the Act. This Act also prohibits price-fixing, boycotts, and allocations of territories through concert of action by competitors. It is also designed to curb the power of corporations with monopoly or near-monopoly positions.

The third major act is the Federal Trade Commission Act, which declares unlawful "unfair methods of competition in commerce, and unfair or deceptive acts or practices in commerce." Specifically, this Act prohibits false advertising and unfair methods of competition which might enable the company to achieve a monopolistic position.

The fourth act grouped among the antitrust laws is the Robinson-Patman Act. It is considered an amendment of the Clayton Act but is generally referred to by its own name. It prohibits discriminations in price where the probable consequences of such discriminations would result in a lessening of competition or a tendency to create a monopoly.

Internal Revenue Service

As the tax collector, the IRS has a continuing interest in mergers and acquisitions. The merger parade of the 1960s developed into a tidal wave in 1967 and 1968. Conglomerates were appearing at a rate commanding the attention of the investing public and the IRS. The Internal Revenue Code of 1954 on tax-free acquisitions held up quite well, but it was the plethora of mergers and acquisitions with what Wall Street called "Chinese money" or "funny money," which exploited loopholes and eroded an important sector of the tax base, that concerned government.

In 1969, Committee Chairman Wilbur D. Mills of the House Ways and Means Committee introduced H.R. 7489 in an attempt to close some of the loopholes in the tax laws affecting mergers and acquisitions. The Tax Reform Act of 1968 was passed by the Congress and signed into law by President Nixon on December 30, 1969. Its many provisions will affect the tax liabilities not only of corporations seeking to acquire other corporations or to merge, but the tax liabilities of individual taxpayers, foundations, real estate interests, oil and mineral interests and every business which once enjoyed an investment credit as well.

A number of the provisions as they affect corporate mergers and acquisitions were mentioned in Chapter 6. There is no question that the Tax Reform Act will be changed by judicial action and by discovery of loopholes by corporate counsel. For the moment, the "Chinese-money" merger game has been checkmated. In time new developments to ease the tax burden will be tried by corporations involved in the merger and acquisition world—all in perfectly legitimate ways—and just as surely, the democratic process operating through the Congress and the executive arms, such as the Internal Revenue Service, will seek to change the course of the new flood tide.

Other Regulatory Agencies

The Internal Revenue Service, the Civil Aeronautics Board, Comptroller of the Currency, and other federal agencies can look over the shoulder of merger-minded companies by exercising a great variety of powers. The case of Financial General Corporation is interesting. This company, operating under exemption from the 1956 Bank Holding Act, acquired a number of banks to gain a position in that field while, at the same time, expanding into mortgage companies, merchant banking, industry and insurance. When the exemption was removed by legislation in 1966, Financial General Corporation, now Financial General Bancshares, was given 12 years in which to dispose of its non-banking assets.

Financial General then went to the Congress for relief for its stockholders from income taxes that would result from the spin off of its non-banking assets. After a long period, the legislation was enacted and the bill signed by the President. The complete plan for the required spin off of assets had to be presented to the IRS and the Federal Reserve Commission, each of which had jurisdiction or cognizance over the disposition of assets. The non-banking assets were placed in a company called Financial Security, which then obtained stockholder approval to merge with International Bank. The entire process took about one week short of three years, and during that period, since the company was enjoined from buying more than 5 percent of any other company, there was no legal way to acquire other companies. This is an involved case admittedly, but it gives some idea of the restrictions that can inhibit any company whose acquisition activities come under government jurisdiction.

State "Blue-Sky Laws"

In cases where the buyer is not required to register his securities with the Securities and Exchange Commission because they are exempt, the state law may, nevertheless, require registration of the buyer's stock with the State Securities Commission. Although many state laws have exemptions similar to those in the Federal law, other states may require registration or notice. To avoid violating these state "Blue-Sky Laws" a buyer should therefore carefully check the laws of any states involved in an acquisition to determine the existence of such requirements for registration.

The strictest law is in California. Before commencement of negotiations with the seller or shareholders to acquire a California company for stock, a buyer must obtain a so-called "negotiating permit" from the Commission of Corporation. In addition, the California Commission of Corporations has required the insertion of a clause in an acquisition contract making the contract unenforceable unless and until the California Division of Corporations issues a further permit authorizing the sale and issuance of the buyer's securities.

Stock Exchange Requirements

The rules of the stock exchange are very explicit about what actions must be taken in an acquisition when the stock of the buying or selling company is listed. Even when cash is employed the stock exchange rules may require certain actions by the buyer or seller which are not necessarily required under the laws of the state of incorporation or under the provisions of the corporate charter.

The New York Stock Exchange company manual says that there must be predisclosure handling of important corporate matters so as to obviate unusual market activity. Companies listed on the New York Stock Exchange are required to keep confidential records of their major acquisitions when circumstances are as indicated in the following rule: "Acquisitions, mergers, stock splits, changes in dividend rates or earnings, new contracts, products for discoveries are the type of developments most likely to be involved. Frequently these matters require discussion and study by corporate officials before final decisions can be made. The extreme care which must be used in keeping such studies and discussions on a confidential basis is evident. The market action of a company's securities should be closely watched at a time when consideration is being given to such matters, so that if the occasion should arise the company would be prepared to make a public announcement of the matter under consideration."

Leaving the Fine Points to Legal Counsel

The foregoing brief discussion is not intended to be comprehensive. Governmental regulation is a legal problem requiring years of study for the legally trained individual. The executive in the acquisition movement should be cognizant of the problem in his business, but not overly worried by the implications. Government action takes place in very probably less than five percent of the total number of acquisitions and mergers annually. Most sophisticated buyers of companies will ask their legal counsels to look at the proposed acquisitions, and if the acquisition appears to have some possible impingement into the area of government regulation, the prudent executive will check the matter out informally with the government agency through his lawyer. However, it should be noted that there is respectable opinion to the effect that this is the worst possible course, since it could invite attention to a matter which might not be considered by the government. Moreover, the odds against government challenge suggest that a "low profile" may be the best policy in many cases.

State legal requirements and those of the major stock exchanges are no bar to the completion of an acquisition, but rather a set of ground rules which must be understood and complied with.

Whenever your actions in the acquisition arena call for disclosure to the public under federal or state regulations or stock exchange rules, be quick to make a public announcement. In this connection, bear in mind that press relations are vitally important in acquisitions. Understandably, negotiators are concerned about secrecy and usually get so wrapped up in the challenge of the give-and-take that when they arrive at a deal they forget to let the public know. But the public and stockholders must be let in on the agreement just as soon as it is signed. The press release usually tells that the "First Lunar Corporation has agreed to purchase the Venus-Mars Corporation for stock." The disclosure of the approximate sale price is a matter for agreement between the principals. If either company's stock is listed on an Exchange, immediate word should be sent so that the information may go onto the Dow Jones ticker.

Meanwhile there are many requirements to be met for full disclosure to the government. The best suggestion is to leave these matters in the capable hands of your corporate secretary and your legal counsel.

Having dealt with governmental regulatory questions, the buyer and seller are then ready to work out their agreement, and a contract.

Checklist on Governmental and Other Considerations in Acquisitions

I. Anti-Trust Legislation

   A. Clayton Act, Section 7

   Where a corporation acquires assets or stock in another corporation and the effect of the acquisition may be substantially to lessen competition or to tend to create a monopoly, the act is violated.

   B. Sherman Act

   Provides that "every contract, combination in the form of trust or otherwise, or conspiracy, in restraint of trade or commerce . . . . is declared to be illegal."

   C. Federal Trade Commission Act

   Provides that "unfair methods of competition in commerce, and unfair and deceptive acts or practices in commerce" are unlawful. This Act prohibits, in addition to false advertising, unfair methods of competition which, if permitted to grow unchecked, might enable a company to achieve a monopolistic position.

   D. Robinson-Patman Act

   This amendment to the Clayton Act prohibits discriminations in prices where the probable consequences would be either a substantial lessening of competition or a tendency to create a monopoly.

II. Securities and Exchange Commission

   Unless a registration statement is in effect with the SEC, it is unlawful for any person to use any means of interstate commerce, including the mails, to sell any security. There are certain exceptions to this broad rule:

   1. Where cash is used.
   2. Many types of securities such as municipal, state and federal securities are exempt.
   3. A non-public offering may be exempt when the stock of the seller is closely held.
   4. Rule 133. Statutory mergers, or when the circumstances indicate there will be no "sale," "offer," "offer to sell," or "offer for sale."

III. Internal Revenue Service

   A. "Tax-free" mergers and acquisitions, under Reorganizations "A", "B" and "C".

   B. Taxable acquisitions through use of cash, notes, bonds, debentures, warrants or any combination of these methods of purchase.

IV. Other Federal Regulatory Agencies
   A. FCC, for the communications industry.
   B. ICC, for the transportation industry.
   C. CAB, for the airlines.
   D. Federal Reserve Board and Controller of the Currency, for banks and savings and loan businesses.

V. Stock Exchange
   Disclosure rules for any significant business action taken by listed companies.

VI. State "Blue Sky" Laws
   State requirements for registration of an acquisition or merger, in cases where no SEC registration is required.

VII. Insider Rules
   SEC and Common Law requirements that insiders such as officers, directors or controlling stockholders will not take advantage of inside information for their own benefit in connection with an acquisition.

Chapter 9

HOW TO REACH A BASIC AGREEMENT, PREPARE A CONTRACT, AND CLOSE THE INITIAL AGREEMENT

Getting Together

The negotiations, initial meeting and plant tour, and careful analysis of governmental regulations which might govern the merger or acquisition are now out of the way and the time has come to reach a "basic agreement." This is best done during a meeting of the buyers and sellers. It is advisable not to have too many people present at this meeting, which may be the third, fourth, or more between the principals. In fact, the lawyers, accountants, tax experts, and other advisers are best left out, since their professional advice could complicate what is essentially a mutual understanding between the top managements of both parties. If the meeting can be held to two or three persons from each side, there is a much better chance of freely discussing the basic points of the agreement and of having both the buyer and the seller take part in writing the agreement.

The Agreement,

The initial agreement, which should be limited to about three pages, may include the purchase price in dollars or in stock, the interest rates to be paid on any monies involved, and the escrow agreements. Any employment agreements with the chief executive and his key personnel may also be noted, although this should be limited, if possible, to no more than four or five executives. The agreement might say something along the following lines:

> The Potomac Corporation hereby offers to purchase from the Missouri Corporation 730,000 shares (100%) of the issued and outstanding $1 par value common stock of the Missouri Corporation, a Nebraska corporation, for $4,200,000 on the terms and conditions set forth below.

Often, the buyer has a tendency to assume that when the price is settled the deal is completed. This is not the case at all. In fact, there are many specifics, including employment agreements and a possible change of location, that may have to be dealt with. In one example, a seller said that no matter what was paid for his company and no matter how good a parent the buyer turned out to be, he did not want to leave the city of Nashville. Thus, if there was any thought of changing the location of business, the prospective buyer could forget the deal.

Another negotiation faltered and almost died when the acquiring company demanded that the owner-seller give up the yacht he had enjoyed for several years. The problem of perquisites, such as cars, country club memberships, and the like, can become one of the most troublesome problems in any negotiation. They are rarely placed on the table during the initial negotiations and usually are considered of such minor importance that proper attention is not given to them.

Human Factors

From a human relations viewpoint it is good business to permit the chief executive, particularly the owner, of a firm being acquired to retain his position and prestige in the community. To his neighbors and his friends he is "Mr. Big" of the XYZ Corporation and his place in the community depends on how his company operates. It is certainly demeaning if as soon as a firm is acquired, the company's signboard comes down or is repainted to show that it is a subsidiary or division of a larger company. Surely, there is a more diplomatic way to indicate the acquired company's new status. The same problem arises with company stationery. Careful consideration should be given to having the acquired company overprint the name of the acquiring company on letterheads and other official items of stationery. A wiser course might be to use something like the following, and in small type: "A Division (or Subsidiary) of Majority Enterprises, Inc."

The cost of the perquisites enjoyed by the chief executive usually is an insignificant amount compared to the purchase price, and it may be a cheap enough investment in good will. If the acquiring company is so set in its policy that it cannot accept the unusual perquisites, or does not want to give the owners of subsidiary companies anything that is not given to other executives of the parent corporation, then it is well to state this at the beginning of the negotiations. These matters should be thoroughly understood because they can be like the sand in the valve that spoils the smooth operation of the engine.

The Matter of Costs and Fees

Another problem that has caused considerable difficulty in negotiations is the brokerage fee mentioned earlier. Usually, the broker is asked to submit a letter of authorization from the president of the company that is for sale, as well as notification that the seller will pay the brokerage fee. If that is the agreement, it should be discussed early in the negotiations so that it is known and understood by both sides. Occasionally the question of fee is presumably resolved early in negotiations, but is raised again when the seller discovers that the fee, perhaps as much as $50,000 or $100,000 is more than he expected. He may suggest that it be divided equally among the parties, or be added to the purchase price. Here again it would be wise for the buyer to know exactly what his company's position is so that should this sticky question arise, he will know whether to compromise or be adamant. Either way, neither a brokerage fee disagreement nor perquisites should be allowed to stall what is a reasonable and equitable acquisition. In terms of percentages, the two together should not amount to more than 3 percent or 4 percent of the total purchase price and they should be discussed openly by the purchasers to determine whether they are acceptable as an additional cost of doing business. The buyers also must recognize that there will be significant legal, auditing, and printing costs.

Any acquisition, even a small one, will cost a minimum of $100,000 for fees and services, plus a good deal more for the time and effort contributed by the executives of the company. To this will be added travel expenses and the costs of any special studies that are made. Case in point: one $2 million acquisition had a brokerage fee of $75,000, legal fees of $35,000, auditing fees of $10,000, and other purchasing costs of $10,000, for a total of $130,000. Another cost which is often justified is a survey of the product line and marketing setup of the prospective acquisition. In some cases, companies will make these studies and then decide not to buy. These studies are of considerable help and could prove of great worth to anyone else looking at the company should the deal fall through.

The Contract

In recent years, when acquisition agreements have been accomplished at a rapid rate, a general pattern has evolved; the formal contract often extends from 125 to 150 pages and there are usually about 11 general sections, each of which is needed. It should be remembered that each acquisition contract should reflect the details of that particular transaction since these will be different in every case.

In the general contract pattern outlined below, it is necessary to point out that it covers stock-for-stock transaction and would have to be altered for acquisitions involving cash or a combination of stock and cash.

General State of Agreement

Most acquisition contracts begin with a general statement of the transaction stating that the buyer and the seller desire to enter into an agreement and plan of reorganization with each other under which the seller, for cumulative convertible preferred stock without par value, will convey and transfer to the buyer certain assets, and that the buyer will acquire from the seller all of the seller's rights, title, and interest in and to all of the properties and assets of the seller covered by the agreement, including but not limited to cash, money on deposit, the good will of the business, and the right to and use of its name, tradenames, and trademarks, customer lists, credit and sales records, and all other interests which the seller has any right to by ownership, use, or otherwise. And, importantly, the buyer will assume all the liabilities of the seller, except as provided hereafter.

Representations and Warranties of Seller

The representations and warranties of the seller contained in the contract concern all aspects of his business and they generally will be the same whether the buyer acquires assets or stocks of a seller. These statements and warranties enable the buyer to obtain additional information about the seller's company and give the buyer legal protection should the facts represented and warranted prove false. Where the seller's business also includes one or more subsidiaries, the representations and warranties on the status of the seller's business should also include such subsidiaries.

The most important representation and warranty would regard the financial statement. This can be handled through the use of an audit, and the contract and the sale price may be made conditional on what the audit shows.

There should also be a representation about income tax, stating that all proper returns for taxes have been filed by the seller and when the Internal Revenue Service last approved the tax situation of the company. The language might state that the seller's "income tax liability has been finally determined by the Internal Revenue Service." It should be noted that even after an audit by the Internal Revenue Service, unless a closing agreement has been signed or the statute of limitations has run out, additional changes in income tax liabilities may occur.

When the seller has government contracts in force, the status of renegotiation proceedings should normally be made a part of the representations.

The next representation should be that the accounts receivable are good and collectable and that the recorded aggregate amounts and reserves for doubtful accounts are accurate. The seller should be required to maintain insurance that is in force at the time of the negotiations.

All inventions and disclosures of improvements on products should be included in a representation. It is possible that the seller might not wish to disclose certain inventions prior to the closing, but would prefer to make due notices in the final disclosure of inventions and the accompanying representations.

Finally, the seller would make in the closing document a statement and representation as to the condition of business, particularly with reference to the fact that no significant adverse changes have taken place in the business as the result of transactions during the period of negotiations.

Representations and Warranties of the Buyer

Normally the seller will be satisfied if he receives assurance that the stock being paid to him by the buyer is properly authorized, issued and delivered to him. Where the buyer pays the seller in cash, usually no assurances or representations are needed. Where the buyer pays the seller in stock and the seller signs an "investment" letter, the seller properly may seek representations and warranties from the buyer concerning the condition of the buyer's business.

The buyer may also be required to warrant that the acquisition does not violate any loan agreements such as on his long-term debt to insurance companies or banks. The statement would be to the effect that the buyer is not subject to any charter, by-law, mortgage, lien, lease, agreement, instrument, order, judgment, or decree, or any other restriction of any kind or character that would prevent consummation of the transaction contemplated by this agreement, provided the holders of its capital stock approve the creation of the convertible preferred stock issuable in the transaction. The warrant would also state that the consummation of the transaction will not result in the breach of any term or provision, or be a default under any indenture, mortgage, deed of trust, or other agreement.

Assets to be Acquired by the Buyer

When purchasing the stock of a company, the definition of assets to be acquired is fairly simple. However, where the buyer acquires other assets, particularly if the assets do not constitute all the assets but only a portion, the definition of property may be complicated. There should be in this case a definition of exactly what land, buildings, machinery, and equipment, office furniture and fixtures, nonexpendable dyes, inventories, prepaid items such as insurance, and prepaid royalties and patents and patent applications, and other assets should be clearly defined. It is necessary on occasion to get an outside appraisal of certain assets and a third-party appraisal can be useful to both sides. It should be added that the seller's tax- free fund claims, if any, should be excluded from the assets of the business.

Payment of a Purchase Price

The purchase price is usually a fixed number of dollars or a stated number of shares of stock. On other occasions a formula may define the amount of cash or stock that the buyer will pay, sometimes on a deferred or contingency basis.

The price of the inventory is subject to a good deal of negotiation since the value of inventories varies according to the valuation methods. The raw material usually is the easiest part to evaluate, but work in process and finished goods are difficult to price because they are dependent upon other factors which make it difficult to come to a quick and easy decision.

Buyer's Assumption of Liabilities

When the buyer acquires stock of the selling company, he also assumes the liabilities of the corporate business since there is no change in the entity. On the other hand, when the buyer acquires the assets for cash, he leaves the liabilities to the seller, unless there is a specific exclusion in the contract. In the latter case, the buyer should receive assurances that there are no liens attaching to the assets, such as mechanics or materialmen liens, for example.

Seller's Indemnification of the Buyer

When the buyer does not assume all of the liabilities of the selling company, the seller usually agrees to indemnify the buyer against unassumed liabilities, which may be contingent or otherwise. The indemnity clause is a continuation of other clauses in the contract that fix the obligation assumed by the buyer.

Seller's Conduct of the Business Pending Closing

The contract usually restricts the seller from certain actions during the period between the contract's signing and the closing date. It also usually requires the seller to conduct the business in an ordinary way, though there often is some reservation that he can check with the buyer in the event that some unusual action is needed to keep the business in operation. There are occasional exceptions such as the payment of the next regular dividend, or certain capital expenditures that had been scheduled for the period between the contract's signing and closing.

Conditions Precedent to the Closing

The possible conditions precedent to the closing may be certain rulings by the Commissioner of Internal Revenue as to the tax-free status of the transaction. There may also be a statement of conditions precedent to the closing that have to do with the correctness of the buyer's or seller's representations. Also, the purchase is contingent on the seller furnishing the buyer with certified copies of certain resolutions and other certified documents necessary to complete the contract.

The Plan of Reorganization

The acquisition contract should contain a clear statement indicating which of the parties is to pay the brokerage commission, and providing that each party indemnify the other from payment of commissions which the indemnifying party has caused to become due and payable.

General Provisions

There may be other provisions in the contract detailing the mechanics of giving notice, including a clause requiring the buyer to keep the results of his investigation confidential. If the parties have some reason to believe that governmental action may be taken to block the proposed acquisition, they provide for such contingencies in the acquisition contract. A subsequent clause might provide for a postponement of the closing date if some unexpected difficulty arises.

The legal staff should also investigate applicable state taxcs. In some cases, where the normal corporate taxes do not apply, a state may impose a compensating use tax. Under the circumstances, there should be provision in the contract for the buyer or seller to pay such tax. Also, if employment contracts are to be signed coincident with the closing, these too should be covered at this point.

There are a host of other possible situations which the lawyers will normally look into and possibly cover in the contract, such as any special notice that should be taken of employee benefit plans, stock option plans, collective bargaining agreements, security clearances, classified documents, bank accounts, and customer contracts.

Usually, a contract contains a covenant that the seller will not compete with the buyer. From the buyer's point of view, if he is vulnerable under antitrust laws, he must weigh the economic value of the covenant against the legal implications.

Finally, the contract's provisions should make certain that all the loose ends are wrapped up, that the business can continue and that the payment is correct down to the last cent based on the appraisal of fixed assets, evaluation of inventory, and any other assets or liabilities which would affect the final purchase price.

Along with the contract there will be a host of exhibits, including such items as the financial statements of the seller, a list and description of all real property, a list of machinery and equipment, a list of patents, patent applications, trademarks, and copyrights, a list of contracts, agreements, and leases, a description of any litigation pending, the names of stockholders who are authorized to sign investment letters, and a list of suppliers and customers.

The executive charged with supervising acquisition normally will not read the entire contract, nor will he be concerned with many of the items. In fact, many items will be exclusively the province of the legal staff. It is the responsibility of the supervising executive to make certain that matters being debated by the legal staffs of the buyer and seller do not become difficulties which may inhibit the negotiation altogether. For the most part, the relationship between the lawyers of the buyer and seller are amicable and any disagreements usually are worked out quite satisfactorily and without undue difficulty.

The Closing

"There is no deal until the papers are signed," cautions an old adage, and the statement holds as true for mergers and acquisitions as for any other business transaction. Sometimes both the buyer and seller will sign the acquisition contract and close the deal all in the same day. While not usual, such speed is possible, and in some cases preferable, where there are no conditions delaying the closing, such as tax rulings or Securities and Exchange Commssion opinions.

Executing the Contract

When the buyer is purchasing certain selected assets of the seller for cash, the execution of the contract and the closing are preferably simultaneous. This is especially pertinent if the inventories are part of the transaction and the price of the inventories depends on a physical count, which is also made simultaneously.

Occasionally, when it is advantageous to sign the contract and close simultaneously, but when certain information is not available in advance, the legal staffs will have the buyer and the seller agree in advance on the general language of the acquisition contract in its entirety and on the form of the closing documents. Blanks will be left for certain items, such as the price of the inventory. This approach permits the buyer and seller jointly to take a physical inventory of the seller's assets and fix the price to be inserted in the contract. In some cases, even this item may be left until later, pending the certified figure for the price of the inventory.

In an acquisition where the closing is contingent upon rulings or approval of stockholders, or the listing or registering of stock with the stock exchange or the Securities and Exchange Commission, the completion of certain items in the contract may be delayed. It may be necessary for the U.S. Department of Justice to rule on the deal from an antitrust point of view; the seller may have conditioned his closing upon obtaining a ruling from the Internal Revenue Service that the transaction is to be treated as a tax-free acquisition; or the contract may require the buyer to register his shares with the Securities and Exchange Commission, or to list newly issued shares on the stock exchange. In such circumstances, the parties have to sign the acquisition contract in advance and stipulate sufficient time prior to the actual closing for the contract conditons to be met. In such situations the closing may take place as much as three or four months later.

Anticipating Difficulties

Additional problems may arise when stock registration is necessary. For example, the required registration statement must be prepared, including financial data satisfactory to the Securities and Exchange Commission, and this may consume a considerable period of time. In addition, after the registration statement is prepared, there will be a period of time before it becomes effective. In such cases, as soon as the acquisition contract is signed, the buyer normally should begin preparation of the registration statement so that it can be expected to become effective within the period specified in the contract. It is normal to allow from 60 to 90 days after the signing of the acquisition contract for the registration statement to become effective. The registration statement, called the "S-1", must contain a great deal of information, such as the plan of distribution, the use of proceeds by the registrant, sales other than for cash, the capital structure, summary of earnings, and a description of the business and the property. There also must be a listing of pending legal proceedings, long-term debt, other securities, names of the directors and executive officers and their remuneration, the options to purchase securities, and the names and amount held of the principal holders of security. Also required is the interest of management and others in certain transactions, and, finally, the complete financial statements.

If Done Right, the Going Is Smooth

A detailing of all the specific requirements for closing may create the incorrect impression that it is a difficult task and one that may hamper the closing of the deal. Actually in most cases, the principals of the buying and selling companies do not have much to do with the closing, since this is the responsibility of the legal staffs. In many cases, the principals do not attend the closing because as far as they are concerned the acquisition has been completed at this point. They simply turn over the formality of signing the documents to their representatives. Nevertheless, there usually are a great number of documents which must be signed by the chief executive and he should be prepared for a rather long signature session during which he will be signing lengthy documents that will be too long to read. However, it is a good idea to read the completed document because it may yield ideas for future deals, as well as specific points which should be considered for the next acquisition contract.

Most closings are conducted at a bank or a lawyer's office at a specified date and time. Certain payments are made and the lawyers make certain that all contract provisions have been met and that all documents are passed from one party to the other at the proper time.

Normally, if the companys' stocks are listed on any stock exchange, the affected exchange is notified immediately that the closing has taken place.

Once the closing has been completed, the next problems have to do with the human relations involved in integrating the seller's employees and his business into the parent organization. This is a time for quick action and some of the things which might be done will be discussed in the following chapter.

Chapter 10

SUCCESSFUL HANDLING OF POST-MERGER ADJUSTMENT

The Case of Omark Industries and KSM Products, Inc.

The *Wall Street Journal* commenting on the post-merger adjustment problems arising from the 1966 acquisition of KSM Products, Inc. by Omark Industries, Inc., stated: "Like brides and grooms, companies that marry must learn to live together, and the period of adjustment is often painfully difficult and surprisingly long."

The consolidation of Omark, an Oregon timber harvesting equipment maker, and KSM, a New Jersey manufacturer of welding equipment and industrial fasteners, snarled some sales and manufacturing operations, sent travel and telephone bills soaring, forced extensive realignment of management responsibilities, and caused morale-damaging confusion among employees. Standardization of accounting practices, cost controls, advertising efforts, and employment policies proved to be a Herculean task. As the former sales manager for KSM put it, "Nobody told us it would be easy, but we never thought it would be this tough."

Omark made five other acquisitions after it bought KSM and John D. Gray, chairman and chief executive officer, observed that Omark "learned something new" in making each of these acquisitions. He added that the company's problems with KSM made later consolidations easier. For one thing, Omark learned to estimate the costs of the getting-acquainted period more accurately. Gray stated: "Accountants, engineers, and executives of Omark and KSM ran up $40,000 in travel bills consolidating the departmental operations. Telephone bills between Portland and Moorestown, New Jersey totalled more than $3,000 the first three months."

A Whole New Ball Game

Amalgamations and assimilations cause considerable reevaluation in any company. Some companies for example, feel that all employee and fringe benefit policies should be standardized, whereas others accept the fact that the situation is different in each case and leave this area pretty much as it is. In quite a number of cases when purchasing privately owned or small publicly owned companies, the new owner finds there is no pension plan or profit-sharing plan. Thus, one of the first moves must be to induce management to make a study and prepare recommendations for the future. It is probably a mistake for the acquiring company to assume that conditions in Georgia, Nebraska, or Michigan are similar, and that the situations confronting companies in widely scattered areas are the same. A good case can be made for permitting the former owners and managers to determine what the employees think is best for that company and for allowing them to work out a plan which is somewhat similar, but not necessarily exactly the same, as the one used by the acquiring company. The problem is undoubtedly more complicated if the company is to become a division rather than a subsidiary. In the latter case, it is usually easier to permit the company to operate almost autonomously.

The Omark-KSM merger is not intended as a "horrible" example since it is not unusual. When the news of a merger appears on the Dow-Jones ticker, the report often sends the stocks of both companies to new highs. The stockholders' vote is usually overwhelmingly in favor of a well- conceived merger. Most mergers seem to be logical partnerships and there is the belief that the result will be more rapid growth together than could have been achieved separately.

Well-planned mergers are usually successful – ultimately. The honeymoon of hope and promise does not last long because an awareness of mutual problems dawns quickly. Experienced executives know that there are risks. The signing of the purchase contract is only the beginning, not the end. After legal and financial merger comes the complicated job of fitting two different organizations together. Each company has a different style of leadership, different structure, habits, values, methods of operating– all of which, and more, vary considerably from one company to another.

Getting At the Central Problem of Human Relations

When a merger is contracted, the president of the acquiring company is faced with an immediate sales job. He can expect to address a meeting of the acquired company's employees, during which he should be sincere in his praise and assurances. He should promise a brighter future in a larger and more profitable company and attempt to dampen insecurity. Usually he will state, and truthfully, that no changes are contemplated. Business will go on as before.

The rank-and-file worker is not as likely to be affected as the executive, except in the rare case when plants are shut down or moved, or when a wildcat strike ensues.

The larger and more immediate problem is with the executive team. As one displaced manager told an executive recruiting firm, "Most mergers are based on purely financial considerations. This means that not only is too little thought given to people, but frequently a conscious effort is made to eliminate them."

One financial vice president, the victim of consolidation after a merger, said bitterly, "I wish now that they'd just fired me in the first place."

A veteran of a half-dozen acquisitions reacted this way, "I'd have been upset and angry also if I had lost my job because I was on the receiving end of a merger. However, there is another side to the coin." He explained that the acquisition group rarely sees the management team of the acquired company more than a half dozen times. "It isn't possible to evaluate people's abilities when you see them on parade. It's only when you see them under stress and meeting challenges that you can get a true estimate."

Furthermore, the acquiring company will make preliminary judgments about possible changes in the management, marketing, manufacturing, and financial functions in the company being purchased, but when confronted by the actual operating situation the preliminary evaluation may not apply.

Digging for the Facts Pays Off

Edward M. Scheu, Jr., president of Good Humor Corporation, believes that pre-acquisition studies are vital. He reports that when Lipton was considering the purchase of Good Humor, specific reports were made on company operations and future plans. The reports took a good deal of digging and thought, but when the deal was consummated they saved a lot of time. Lipton's president, W. Gardner Barker, states, "Developing such a report may take us a little longer to complete the deal, but once it is accomplished, we don't have to spend six months trying to find out what we really bought and where we really want to go."

Three fundamental tasks appear to be important in the post-merger period:

1. Deciding on centralized or decentralized control of the acquired company;
2. Integrating the functions of the business, including financial, marketing, manufacturing, industrial relations, research and administration;
3. Building for greater profitability and expansion.

Centralized or Decentralized Control

The decision on the method of control for the absorbed company can be determined in large part before the contract is signed. The acquiring company's organizational history will largely determine the pattern, though there will always have to be some blending of desires and realities.

Large diversified companies and conglomerates often insist that the total financial function be centralized and carried out at headquarters, and many acquisition-minded companies believe that this is the most efficient method of handling this function. In one situation, the financial vice president of a small company which was sold to a giant read in the press release that there would be no changes. Within a month, a directive arrived stating that all financial records would be picked up and taken to the central office. The financial vice president started searching for a new job immediately. The situation could have been avoided if the owner-manager had raised the issue before the merger by asking for an employment contract for his financial vice president and a clarification of how the financial function was to be handled.

The Proper Stance of Management

No acquired company president should be nonplussed or cowed when dealing with a big company with a highly centralized organization. The signs are there for him to read, but too often his desire to make a favorable sale clouds his vision. In such situations, the president may ask for protection for four or five of his key officials, but even that assurance, backed up by employment contracts, will not guarantee that these executives will have the same kind of jobs they previously enjoyed.

Centralized firms are looking for efficiency and profits. They see in a merger an opportunity to widen the scope of their managers and expect that the role of the acquired company's management will be subordinate.

A small company in the South owned by two men was courted in an acquisition effort by a giant conglomerate. Teams of accountants, engineers, and marketing men combed through the company operations. The owners, seeing the handwriting on the wall, called off the merger negotiations and looked for an acquisition-minded company with a basic belief in decentralized operations. Thus, many of the problems resulting from mergers, particularly the vital human problems, are the result of not making clear the decision on control early in the negotiations.

The decision to adopt a decentralized operation may occur when the product line and marketing approach of the seller are quite different from those of the buyer. An autonomous operation is more difficult to control, but it offers greater potential growth. A good organization given the confidence of the acquiring company will more often than not produce greater results than one which is strictly guided and controlled.

Convincing the Right People

Under a decentralized approach, the big problems are communication and coordination. The key word is persuasion. On the surface a good case can be made for the decentralized setup of joining two companies. However, if the "purchased" management is allowed to go on in the old way, there are bound to be pitfalls. The major problem is to show the acquired company how the larger company can open doors by providing working capital and improving marketing and manufacturing efficiency.

Acquiring companies sometimes use the device of putting one of their key management men into the acquired company to assist in its development. He should be someone who is loyal and enthusiastic in his support of the parent company and, preferably, someone who has participated in the merger proceedings. Most importantly, he should be someone who is personally acceptable and who can contribute to the solution of problems.

Integrating Functions

How can two organizations be integrated? Normally top managers on both sides of a merger usually ask for time to avoid precipitate action. Moreover, success in integration comes only through a managed process. One approach is for top executives from both companies to act as a joint planning task force, requiring that all contact between the companies be through this group. Assuming that executives are conscientious and eager to achieve efficiency and economy, the problem is one of directing their efforts toward reconciling the two different systems of operation to prevent mixups and crises.

Decision confronting the control group may be broken down into immediate "must" actions and those that can be put aside for a time. Pressing decisions vary in each merger and depend on how well the companies meld together. If there is little compatibility in sales and marketing, or in manufacturing, these functions can be left for later evaluation and decision. The more pressing financial problems can be tackled at once.

In one case, a company was acquired because it had products and a sales organization that complemented those of the parent company. The sales vice president moved in immediately to organize the marketing setup. There were shifts in personnel, changes in the promotion ladder, and dozens of other disturbing and morale-debasing actions. The situation could have been foreseen by the sales vice president, and prior planning could have avoided many of the points of friction.

A decentralized parent company makes a merger with more ease than a centralized, highly organized company. The former can assure the president and his immediate top management staff that operations remain in their hands and changes will come slowly. In such acquisition situations, the parent company can take a hands-off attitude about hiring and firing as long as the company continues to be profitable. One acquired company lost its financial vice president because at the time of the acquisition, he made money out of the sale of his stock and decided to move into land development, a major interest for some time. The president of the company called the chief executive of the acquiring company saying that he would like to send up his selection for the financial spot for an interview. The chief executive wisely declined, saying, "If I put my stamp of approval on the man, you may be reluctant to let him go if he doesn't measure up. No, I prefer that you make the selection since yours is the responsibility for fielding a profit-making team."

Financial Department

The heads of the financial departments have undoubtedly met during the merger negotiations. The firm being acquired has furnished exhaustive data about its assets and liabilities and methods of accounting. Once the merger becomes fact, the question arises, "How much integration is necessary?"

In the financial sphere, it can be expected that the selling company will have to make weekly and monthly reports of its activities, particularly sales, earnings, backlogs in inventory, receivables, and accounts payable. And, it can be expected to report on labor and sales costs. One good form is a monthly report which compares the present period with the same period of the year before and which shows the cumulative totals for both years. Such a statement would include all the above items plus the backlog and, if possible, projections for the future. It would be expected that one of the first items would be a budget and projections for the remainder of the year, as well as a projection for the following year. This would provide a basis for further discussions between the executives of the two firms.

Among the most immediate and pressing problems is the different ways in which items in the balance sheet are treated. For inventory, some companies use the last-in, other the first-out method of accounting. Research is expensed by some companies; others capitalize it. Pension plans can be treated in several different ways. In one case involving a privately owned company, there was a dispute over the receivables from company officers; the practice of the acquired company had been to lend the officers money for necessities, even for the purchase of homes. The acquiring company, with a strong policy, frowned on such practices.

Sound Accounting Practices and Procedures

Accounting practices are baffling to the uninitiated. Investment tax credits are amortized over the estimated life of the related plant and equipment in some cases; in others, the credits are allowed to "flow through" as a reduction of income taxes. In addition, depreciation may be treated in many different ways. Moreover, the expert in one company may be accustomed to handling things his way and any suggestion that his method is incorrect can result in erosions of good will between the two companies. The decentralized company may let the financial methods stand and make changes gradually. The centralized company may say, "This is the way it will be done."

Marketing

The exceptional case is the one previously mentioned in which the acquired company has products and a sales organization that complement the parent. More often this is not the case and the only recourse is for the president of the parent company to confer with both sales vice presidents to work out a desirable solution.

Usually there is no related sales effort. Since the acquiring firm is larger, it undoubtedly has resources and know-how useful to the acquired company. Promotion, advertising, and sales organization methods that may be superior can be brought to the attention of the "acquired" president and sales vice president gradually over a period of months. The most successful solution is to challenge the initiative of the sales manager, inducing him to come to the parent company for advice on how to solve problems and increase his sales effort.

Manufacturing

Given some similarity in products, the common approach to merged manufacturing is to seek to accomplish the greatest economy and efficiency. If the parent company manufactures every component in its product line and the acquired company has concentrated more on assembly, depending on sub-contractors for most of its components, difficulties may arise. The word of caution here is to proceed slowly with changes. The profit picture of the absorbed company may have been built on sub-contract and assembly work; a sudden shift to a more complete manufacturing role may cause imbalances and disturb the profit pattern.

Engineering advice often is needed by the acquired company, but any basic changes should be made slowly and only after joint discussion. No one can say that one company's manufacturing practices are best; the key is what works best for a particular company. It should be noted in this connection that a major manufacturing benefit of the diversified corporation is that often one company or division can produce items for others. In case of a strike at one company, the others can pitch in to help meet the most pressing requirements.

In one good example of an orderly manufacturing changeover, an acquiring company had put in numerical controls and computerized inventory throughout its plants. The process was studied carefully and the changes made over a period of several years. When its engineers visited the new acquisition's plants, they found what they considered to be an inefficient and old-fashioned manufacturing setup. Proper human relations required the engineers to try to be helpful, while not appearing to be "know-it-alls." The modernization of the acquisition took three years and careful counselling, but it was accomplished without disrupting the profit picture and everyone was pleased.

In another acquisition, it was quickly apparent that a privately owned company just acquired had a very slow turnover of inventory; well above the industry average, in fact. The matter was brought to the vice president of manufacturing in a constructive manner and he was quick to see how he could move his inventory faster, thus freeing funds for working capital. By his own admission, the matter had never before been presented to him in that context.

Industrial Relations

When the parent company is unionized and the acquisition is not, points of friction are certain to arise. Wage rates may be different; work habits are almost certain to vary.

How One Executive Learned the Hard Way

An executive writing in *Dun's Review* told of his traumatic experience in industrial relations. "The news came over the ticker, Everett Products, the electrical-components manufacturer where I was vice president of industrial and public relations, had agreed to merge with General Consolidated, Inc. (GCI), a rapidly diversifying chemical company on an acquisitions binge. Everett was to be a wholly owned subsidiary, and there were to be no management changes.

"At the time of the merger, I thought my position at Everett was as solid as it could be. At 41, I had achieved my career objective. I was responsible for all industrial relations programming throughout the company, which operated 29 factories in the United States and Canada. I was in charge of all personnel administration, fringe benefits, labor negotiations, wage and hour matters, NLRB problems, arbitration cases, community and public relations, some training and plant safety.

"All went well in the merger for about two months. Then, in one move after another, there seemed to be a conscious effort on the part of visiting parent-company vice presidents to diminish the industrial relations role. The first move from GCI was to ask for an outline of all industrial relations responsibilities and functions and to prepare new job descriptions for the Everett staff. Then came the directive to merge the Everett industrial relations department with that at GCI."

The Everett vice president was made "number two" and the former deputy at GCI was let go. Furthermore, the GCI head of industrial relations had been manager, not vice president, and it galled him that his new assistant had been a vice president. He studiously avoided introducing him as a former Everett official. The climax came when the Everett vice president was thrown into a labor relations situation that resulted in a strike. The GCI executive pointedly shoved aside his new assistant and arranged a settlement. The only recourse for the frustrated former Everett official was to resign in disgust.

One disenchanted seller of a company reacted to the post-merger situation this way: "I came to think of myself as a mushroom. During the negotiations I was covered with fertilizer. During the early post-merger and consolidation phase, I was kept in the dark. And finally, after a period, I was canned."

In all the other functions of a manufacturing firm—research, administration and legal—the same kinds of merger problems exist. And, at the heart of most of these problems are pride and prestige, cornerstones of industrial human relations. Many points of friction can be avoided by knowledgeable, experienced executives operating under the tight control of the president of the acquiring company.

Profitability and Expansion

An acquisition-minded company has the two-fold objective of profitability and expansion. At the first meeting of a recently acquired building products company in the Midwest, the newly organized board of directors discussed possible areas of expansion consistent with profitability. Sitting around the table were three members of top management from the acquired company who had been named to the board. The sole question was: "Now that we are merged, we would like to know what ideas you managers have for the expansion of the business."

By the close of the lengthy meeting, a three-fold plan of expansion had been agreed upon. It included the following: (1) The company's profits must continue to increase to give the financial base for expansion; (2) The acquiring company would use its greater financial backing and experience to help make the expansion possible; (3) the expansion program would include a joint venture out of the country, the acquisition of a major distribution outlet, and the acquisition of another company to manufacture a product which the company was warehousing and selling.

It was further agreed that if the president and a representative of the parent company could not find the right kind of acquisition, plans would be drawn for the purchase of the necessary machinery and space to establish the new manufacturing line.

As a result of that meeting, the creative energies of the merged companies were released for new endeavors. The top management of the acquired company went away secure in the belief that the opportunities for them and their associates had been considerably widened. They saw in the merger a bigger job and greater prestige for themselves. End result: they put so much energy into their regular functions that the following year was the most profitable in the history of the company. In fact, profits almost doubled on a 25 percent increase in sales. A year later when the expansion program had been put into effect, the management was looking for new worlds to conquer.

Liaison and Cooperation

The problem of liaison with the acquired company is one that must be faced by the chief executive of the acquiring company. One good idea is for the acquiring company president to spend as much time as possible with the chief executive of the purchased company, and to make a special effort to join him at conventions and exhibitions which are relevant to the company. In addition, visits should be made to the plant and offices at fairly regular intervals, with every effort made to get to know the management socially. Most likely, if the executives of both companies developed good relations during the negotiations, a real friendship will grow between them.

You Don't Argue with Success

The real proof of the pudding is in the eating and if the company continues on its projected profitability curve and accomplishes the desired expansion, the acquisition will have been a good one. If there are certain problems that were hidden under the rug, they will eventually expose themselves to plague management of the acquiring company. Then surgery may be necessary. For example, the employment contract may become a problem. The individual concerned may have to be released, or retained as a consultant, and someone else promoted to operate the acquired company. Where the owner or chief executive of the company being acquired is well along in years, it may be desirable to arrange that in his five-year employment contract he will be the chief executive for two years, after which he will become a consultant. A two-year period would permit the former owner or chief executive to work with the chief executive of the acquiring company to determine who among management should be brought up to the chief executive slot.

Acquisition, as we have stressed thus far, proceeds from the first thought within the acquiring company, through the consummation of the deal, to living with the merger and assimilation and integration of the acquired property. If there is a lesson to be learned, it is that acquisition and merger can be a challenging and pleasant occupation. It brings the persons into contact with new industrial situations in other parts of the country, even abroad, gives new insights into people and business situations, and, perhaps, brings back to the executive of the acquiring company a better appreciation of the problems of his own company. He can more easily view his own company's functions once he has considered just what his company is attempting to do and how a potential candidate for acquisition will help him do it. Acquisition gives the opportunity to re-think the company's plans and objectives and may result in some significant and far-reaching changes.

Chapter 11

CONGLOMERATES, MERGER KINGS AND ONE-BANK HOLDING COMPANIES

Conglomerates on the Grow

The most dramatic and revolutionary development in the world of mergers and acquisitions was the rapid rise of the conglomerate corporation.

One of the largest of the conglomerates is International Telephone and Telegraph, which operates telecommunication systems, manages mutual funds, operates bakeries, manufactures glass, builds hospitals, and rents automobiles. In mid-1970, ITT completed its acquisition of Hartford Fire Insurance Company in a deal valued at $1.8 billion—the biggest merger ever to take place in corporate America. Although the deal was officially consummated after a successful exchange offer, the Justice Department filed an anti-trust suit and ITT is required to keep Hartford as a separate entity until the case is resolved. ITT (assets $5.2 billion) effected the merger of Hartford through an exchange offer in which more than 97 percent of the outstanding stock of Hartford was tendered for ITT cumulative preferred stock. The exchange involved one share of ITT stock, $2.25 convertible Series N, for each share of Hartford common. The preferred is convertible into 1.25 common shares of ITT for three years and thereafter into 1.2 common shares, and is callable after seven years at $85 per share.

The Federal Trade Commission, in its statistics of 1968 mergers, estimated that the aggregate assets of companies acquired by merger were between $11 billion and $12 billion, an increase of almost 50 percent over 1967. Moreover, the number of mergers in 1969 increased 37 percent over 1968 and activity during the first quarter of 1970 was at about the same level as a year earlier. Since the conglomerates accounted for more than 80 percent of the assets acquired in 1968, and since the top 200 manufacturing corporations today control about two-thirds of all assets held by corporations engaged primarily in manufacturing, it is understandable that government's foes of "bigness" in business are alarmed. In fact, several members of Congress, fearful that mergers are leading to greater corporate concentration and a possible monopoly of industrial power, asked the Federal Trade Commission to conduct a fact-finding investigation.

Unquestionably there is deep-rooted concern that large, highly centralized business organizations may result in undesirable economic and political power. However, without a thorough-going study it would be premature to conclude that conglomerates fall into the same category as monopolies and other targets of antitrust policy.

A Look at the Record

How did the conglomerate movement get started? What are their objectives? What is their track record on acquisitions and profits, and who are the men who put these conglomerates together?

The new corporate meaning of conglomerate has yet to be included in Webster's dictionary. Few executives admit to running a company with that label, and fewer yet agree on what the word means. James J. Ling, former chairman of Ling-Temco-Vought, Inc. says that the word "as it has been used most frequently, is meaningless and undefinable." Steven J. Ross, president of Kinney Services, Inc., has "not the slightest idea what the term means."

Fred Sullivan, chairman of Walter Kidde & Company, is not the least bit disturbed at being called a conglomerate, while Brewster L. Arms of The Signal Companies is not certain that his company is a conglomerate, even though it is in gas and oil production, aerospace, and owns Mack Trucks.

The word "conglomerate" originally was used in geology to indicate a rock consisting of parts collected from various sources. The Latin root is "glomerare," meaning to wind in a ball. In an upcoming new edition of Webster's, the definition will be written, "widely diversified company, especially a corporation that by merger or purchase acquires other companies whose businesses are quite unrelated to the corporation's primary activity."

It is understandable that executives like G. William Miller of Textron, J.O. Howell, Jr. of Genesco, R.F. Mattler of TRW and Les Warner of General Telephone & Electronics are back-pedaling away from the designation of "conglomerate." They explain that they are multi-industry companies serving multi-markets.

Walter Kidde's Fred Sullivan reminded a group of bank executives that conglomeration is not new; it is just that the pace is faster. The more diversified a company becomes, the more diversified is its range of talents and resources.

It would seem that merger-minded executives will have to stop shying away from the designation and stand up for objective consideration in any legislative efforts likely to affect reasonable and respectable corporate growth.

How It All Began

How did the conglomerates get started? Theodore H. Silbert, President of Standard Prudential Corporation, states that his company grew in 35 years from a commercial finance company to a diversified "department store of finance." Through acquisition of more than 20 companies in related businesses, it became the third largest independent corporation in its field, offering services in accounts receivable, factoring, leasing, consumer finance, mobile homes, mortgages, real estate, time sales and rediscounting.

Silbert adds: "But then, four years ago, our company changed its entire direction. Through a series of eight accomplished or projected acquisitions and mergers, Standard Prudential became a diversified company with subsidiaries operating in such varied fields as spinning yarn, heat-exchange devices, printing fabrics, mining, electromechanical equipment, lawn mowers, telephone plant facilities, shoes, auction sales, and leathers, as well as commercial finance."

According to Silbert, Standard Prudential developed as a "truly diversified" company and then expanded its horizons to become a "truly conglomerate" company.

In some business quarters, executives state a preference for running a simple, uncomplicated one-product business showing a modest profit. They feel this is preferable to tacking the gigantic problems inherent in managing a multi-product, multi-market complex of companies.

Expand or Contract

The fact of life is that the one-line company must grow spectacularly or wither, or be merged with a larger company. In today's business world, the small company cannot afford the extravagant overhead to meet the needs of the market place—such as manufacturing, advertising, legal, tax, financial, personnel, international, public relations, government relations, and computer technology. Furthermore, because of the limited opportunities for advancement they offer, small companies cannot attract or hold talented and ambitious executives anxious to get ahead.

Columnist Art Buchwald took humorous note of the merger mania. He remarked that the average person has no idea what is happening, yet the merger boom could affect everybody in the nation. "What it boils down to is that if you merge an apple company with another apple company, you're violating the anti-trust laws. But if you merge an apple company with a banana company, then you're building a conglomerate, and whether you know it or not, conglomerates are 'in' things to own."

He explained how a conglomerate works, giving the example of a merger of a drugstore in Georgetown with a meat market in Bethesda. "They call it 'The Great American Drug and Meat Co.' They issue stock and the issue is oversold because any company that has the words 'great,' 'American,' 'drug,' and 'meat' in it must have potential.

"In due course," Buchwald continued, "the conglomerate buys an insurance company, a baseball club, a chicken franchise, a bank, and apartment houses. The two entrepreneurs put up $25 and control $3 billion worth of assets, and each is worth $50 million on paper."

Buchwald puts the clincher on the conglomerate development by claiming that if the drugstore or meat market loses the lease on its store, "the whole conglomerate pyramid could fall down. When you get right down to it, that's the only part of their business the partners understand."

Mounting Criticism

Unquestionably, the criticism against conglomerates is mounting. One result could be a law to regulate and standardize incorporation of companies engaged in interstate commerce. One observer who believes this is William L. Cary, former chairman of the Securities and Exchange Commission and presently a Columbia University law professor. Speaking at an American Bar Association symposium on the conglomerate corporation, Cary suggested such a law to overcome wide differences in state incorporation laws, particularly with regard to tender offers.

Cary's view is shared by many who contend that variations in state laws have invited the aggressive tactics of the corporate empire builders. Critics say that conglomerates have exploited the more permissive provisions of some state laws dealing with acquisition procedures and the intent of the corporation.

Laws Under Consideration

Proposals for a federal law governing corporations have been made on numerous occasions over the past 30 years, but despite the record, the time may now be ripe for such legislation. Even now both Congress and the Justice Department are bent on cooling the merger drive and blocking conglomerate-type acquisitions among the nation's 200 largest corporations.

Architect of the Justice Department's efforts is Assistant Attorney General Richard W. McLaren. Under McLaren's guidance, Justice is hitting hard at the anti-trust question of reciprocity, the practice of favoring one's customers in corporate acquisitions. According to McLaren, "We are bound to apply the anti-trust law as it stands. In the case of reciprocity, we do so with the sense that we are very much on the right track."

The Federal Trade Commission is conducting a broad study of the conglomerate merger trend in American industry, which may result in a significant extension of the antitrust laws into this area. The FTC has said that its study would attempt to ascertain "whether new legislation may be necessary to bring the conglomerate-merger movement under control."

What the FTC Can Do

The FTC's authority in this field is undeniable. Recently, it levelled one of the most comprehensive attacks yet undertaken by the government by calling for the Maremont Corporation to divest itself of 40 acquisitions made since 1953. This divestment would reduce Maremont's annual sales by "well over" $100 million; its sales in 1967 were $186 million. Furthermore, FTC recently approved the merger of Hooker Chemical into Occidental Petroleum only after the two firms agreed to limitations on future activities. Such attacks, coupled with government studies, prompted one analyst to say that the conglomerates have lost their wallop as far as the market is concerned.

FTC's most telling salvo in the fight against conglomerates came in late 1969 when it presented a 700-page staff report to the Senate Judiciary Antitrust and Monopoly Subcommittee. The report was presented by Dr. Willard F. Mueller, for nearly eight years chief economist of the Federal Trade Commission and now a University of Wisconsin economist. Dr. Mueller, an outspoken critic of the merger movement, told the subcommittee that conglomerate mergers are pushing the United States toward a centralized, closed economy with the nation's economic power concentrated in the hands of a few hundred corporations. He recommended that the Justice Department increase anti-trust prosecutions in merger cases under Section 7 of the Clayton Act; that FTC and Justice focus on large conglomerate mergers involving takeovers of firms that already hold leading positions in concentrated industries, as well as on the elimination of tax treatment and accounting practices which encourage mergers.

Stating that since World War II "practically all of the increase in the share of industrial assets held by the 200 largest corporations is directly attributable to mergers," Mueller said that present tax laws actually subsidize mergers. He added that generally accepted accounting practices permit merger-active companies to glamorize their profit performance to exploit speculative behavior in a securities market hungry for growth-type companies, even when the growth in no way reflects additions to the nation's capacity to produce goods and services. He also had these criticisms of the growing concentration of corporate assets:

It increases centralization of corporate decision-making and the likelihood that reciprocal selling will short-circuit the disciplining forces of the market;

It enables conglomerates operating in many markets to use excess profits in some markets to subsidize losses in others, either by price cuts or increasing costs;

It results in a contagious effect since less powerful firms feel obligated to merge with others so they will not be snowed under by their conglomerate rivals;

It greatly broadens and extends traditional "communities of interests" among key industrial decision makers, with the ultimate result of a closed economic system in which price and other business decisions become largely immune from the disciplining influence of the market; and

It is bringing about a major transformation in the geographic pattern of corporate control in the nation, which "carries with it a potential for serious economic and social disruption for the communities involved and reflects an erosion in the fundamental design of the anti-trust laws to foster a wide diffusion of corporate control in the American economy."

The FTC staff report made the following recommendations:

1. Revision of existing laws to remove incentives for merger activity that is unrelated to economic efficiency;
2. Elimination by the Securities and Exchange Commission or Congress of accounting practices that misrepresent merger investment costs;
3. Fuller public disclosure of the financial operations of major corporations through stronger reporting requirements; and
4. Revamping of existing law on interlocking directorates.

Meanwhile, the Securities and Exchange Commission has promulgated rules that will have a major effect on the evaluation of the shares of conglomerates. For the first time, conglomerates will be required to report on securities registration forms both sales and contribution to net income of each division accounting for 10 percent or more of total sales. These corporations would also have to report "to the extent possible" the assets employed in each segment of the business.

In addition, the SEC rules will require that "comparable data on revenues and earnings received from foreign sources and from government procurement, or any single customer, also be reported." This would apply to income amounting to 10 percent or more of sales. The purpose of the proposed rules is to make available information which existing security holders and new investors would be able to use to determine the approximate contribution various lines of business within the conglomerate make to the corporation's overall profitability, or lack of it.

Anti-trust Laws

Antitrust laws, at present, are concerned mainly with two kinds of mergers—those between competitors in the same market and those between suppliers and their customers. Conglomerate mergers generally fall outside either of these categories. They involve different geographic areas, concerns in related but not identical fields, or firms with no apparent relationship.

Actually, however, conglomerate mergers can be challenged by the government in at least three possible areas. First, there is the contention that the merger affords the opportunity for reciprocal purchasing. As conglomerates get larger, some minimal amount of reciprocal purchasing is almost certain to develop, even though care has been exercised to avoid it. A second area for challenge is the argument that the purchaser would have entered the field on its own it if were not permitted to acquire a company in the field. Unfortunately, the purchaser's own records can be used to establish this contention if internal studies have been made to investigate this possibility. Finally, there is the contention that the great financial strength of the purchaser will permit the seller to so dominate the market as to introduce an element of unfair competition. All of these arguments have been successful in the past and will undoubtedly be used in the future.

Donald I. Baker, acting assistant chief of the Evaluation Section of the FTC, said of conglomerates that "bigness is neither good nor bad per se." He did add, however, that there appears to be some economic case for a broader policy to limit random absorption of medium-sized firms into large conglomerates. He said that the conglomerate movement represents a trend toward greater concentration and economy, but he expressed doubt that there are any real economies to be achieved by putting a number of disparate enterprises together in a single corporate structure. Whether as an attack on conglomerates themselves, or as an effort to stem the merger tide, the U.S. Attorney General has reported that fiscal 1968 saw a record number of suits challenging business mergers. During this period, the Justice Department filed 20 anti-merger suits, topping by three the previous high set in 1965.

Mr. Baker suggested three possible legislative changes: the first would involve some form of administrative approval for acquisitons by companies that have reached a specified size; the second would require a company above such a specified size to dispose of assets of a comparable value each time it made a new acquisition (which might encourage large conglomerates to evaluate their acquisitions more carefully); and the third would impower Congress to modify the tax provisions to outlaw the exchange of securities without capital gains tax.

Conglomerate in Action

The merger movement that has skyrocketed into a conglomerate explosion has produced some startling combinations: Radio Corporation of America merging with St. Regis Paper Company; INA Corporation, an insurance company, getting together with an airline, World Airways; Teledyne, an electronics company, buying Argonaut Insurance Company; Transamerica Company, a huge financing empire, joining with Metromedia, Inc., a broadcasting enterprise; a carpet maker, Mohasco, Inc., acquiring the plumbing equipment firm American-Standard, Inc.; International Telephone and Telegraph Corporation purchasing Canteen Corporation, one of the big names in vending machines; and RCA's $117 million purchase of F.M. Stamper Company, the frozen prepared foods producer.

Interestingly, not all conglomerators are well-known and bent on making their names greater. One merger king, Tinkham Veale, II, has built up Alco Standard Corporation of Valley Forge, Pennsylvania, swiftly and with due adherence to a successful formula of betting on winners among smaller privately and publicly owned companies. Over a span of nine years, Alco has developed from a chemical company with sales of $5 million a year and earnings of $120,000 to sales of $455 million and profits of $128 million. Alco Standard's acquisitions primarily have been owner-managed companies with sales of $5 million to $10 million Veale permits a great deal of autonomy among the acquired companies and offers only staff assistance in legal and financial fields.

In contrast to the centralized control exercised by many of the aggressive conglomerates, Alco Standard leaves its companies alone as long as they make a profit. Veale makes the former owners his partners and ties them into the company with generous stock options. Following this simple format, in stark contrast to many of the conglomerates, he keeps moving ahead, and estimates that by 1973 sales will be close to $750 million and profits up to $30 million.

The established, well-known conglomerates like Textron, Litton, American Machine & Foundry, AMK, and many others, have had clear sailing for a number of years. But in the market decline of the late sixties, the market prices of many of the conglomerates fell off drastically. The big mutual funds began sneaking back to take another look. Lately, the conglomerates with fundamental values, good management, and no wild accounting practices have been getting the attention they deserve.

They're Not All Winners

Not all the conglomerates, however, have had the same success. In a *Fortune* article, the author told "Why Rain Fell on 'Automatic' Sprinkler." This conglomerate, now

A-T-O. Inc., took over companies at an unbelievably swift pace that "made careful scrutiny impossible" and unpleasant surprises inevitable.

"Automatic" Sprinkler's growth has been so accelerated that even its name is only vaguely familiar to many businessmen. The Cleveland-based company produces such disparate items as electronic instruments, vacuum cleaners, bomb fins, hydraulic equipment, and baseball gloves, as well as sprinkler systems and other fire-protection devices.

Fortune attempted to draw some lessons from the history of "Automatic," which grew explosively from $23 million to $325 million in six years through the acquisition of some 20 companies. Profits rose even more dramatically than sales. Concluded *Fortune,* "The pace was too fast to allow for thorough investigation of merger partners before deals were made, or for proper assimilation of newly acquired companies before management's attention was diverted to other negotiations."

Chairman Harry E. Figgie, Jr., a former management-consultant and vice president of Rockwell Manufacturing Co., kept up a pace that left the investment community breathless. Deal followed deal at a dizzy pace, and the acquisitions grew more and more far out. Figgie is undoubtedly an able man, and given the proper time to assimilate some of the companies and sell off others, he could well have had "Automatic" Sprinkler back on the track as a well-considered, highly profitable conglomerate.

As the *Wall Street Journal* noted, the conglomerates have had their comeuppance. Government trust-busters have begun to limit their previously unrestrained acquisitions, and a bearish stock market has taken much of the air out of their overvalued price-earnings ratios. "Conglomerates have set such super standards for growth in the corporate community that old-line companies that once achieved solid financial successes are being forced to employ balance-sheet razzle-dazzle to please stockholders."

Disenchantment has overtaken the conglomerates as their stock prices have deteriorated. However, it is hard to see anything more than a pause in the merger parade. As the market rebounds, acquisition and merger will continue apace. It is possible however, that the conglomerate wave may recede as diversified companies with related product lines show their worth.

One-Bank Holding Companies

While the conglomerate rage was boiling, a new method for merger and acquisition appeared on the scene.

Commercial banks began to try out the role of the free-wheeling financial conglomerate. Using what amounted to a "loophole" in the Bank Holding Company

Act of 1956, bank after bank created a "one-bank" holding company that permitted it, in theory at least, to diversify into any kind of business it chose, from a diaper service to a steel mill. Scores of banks have moved to form such organizations, and the list reads like a Who's Who in Banking: First National City, Wachovia Bank & Trust Company, Bank of America (the world's largest), and Crocker-Citizens National Bank of California. The usual procedure is for the bank, through the exchange of stock on a one-for-one basis, to create a general business company to hold it. The bank then becomes the holding company's initial investment and the only bank among any number of businesses the company might acquire.

The future of bank holding companies, however, is somewhat cloudy. In December 1970 Congress passed, and the President signed, legislation to regulate bank holding companies. In late January the Federal Reserve Board, as directed by the legislation, proposed preliminary regulations implementing the new law. The regulations detailed 10 specific activities that are so "closely related to banking" as to be permissible for bank holding companies. The board also published proposed procedures for acquisitions by bank holding companies of businesses in the permissible lines.

Under the proposed regulations, bank holding companies could retain or acquire interests in companies that engage solely in one or more of the following activities: making loans for its own account or for the account of others; operating as an industrial bank; servicing loans; acting as a fiduciary; acting as investment or financial adviser; leasing personal property under certain conditions; acting as insurance agent or broker; acting as insurer for the holding company and its subsidiaries; providing bookkeeping or data processing services; making equity investments in community rehabilitation and development corporations.

Next step for the Fed will be a census of bank holding companies—more than 1,200 of them with over $250 billion in assets. It can be expected to concentrate on the 60 or so big non-banking corporations that also own banks.

There will also be a series of hearings—one for each industry banks seek to enter. The end result is to be a set of industry-wide guidelines that would eliminate the need for separate hearings every time a bank wants to move into a new field. The entire process may take up to two years and the final word on diversification will most likely be up to the court.

In the past, the one-bank holding company has been able to diversify into insurance, leasing, computer services, travel bureaus, real estate development and similar financial-oriented activities. Critics of the trend fear such diversification will undermine the bank's fiduciary responsibilities. Proponents contend that the banks must take this course in order to compete with other financial institutions, which are not hampered by rules and regulations.

Under the Bank Holding Company Act, a bank holding company is defined as a concern that owns 25 percent or more of two or more banks. Such a concern is required to register with the Federal Reserve Board, to submit to government regulation, and to refrain from engaging in non-banking enterprises.

One-bank holding companies, on the other hand, generally have been exempt from regulation by the federal banking agencies.

The trend has created open controversy within the banking community itself, and has generated concern on the part of the Federal Reserve Board. One development has been the decision by over 100 representatives of present or proposed one-bank holding companies to form a new organization to be known as the Association of Corporated Owners of One Bank.

Insurance Company Mergers

The insurance industry also is expected to play a major and growing role in acquisitions and mergers, and a sharply increasing number of insurance companies will likely be approached by industrial concerns interested in diversification.

Finance-banking-insurance companies received 26 tender offers from industrial companies in the first half of 1968, compared to only 12 during the same period the year before, and this trend can be expected to continue as long as many insurance companies are selling below asset value. This condition makes the insurance industry stand out compared with industrial firms now selling at multiples of their net worth or book value per share.

Another reason for the attractiveness of insurance companies as corporate acquisitions is the fact that they have a large share of their assets in stocks and bonds. Industrial companies have always viewed insurance company investment portfolios with some awe.

Armand G. Erpf, partner of the investment house of Loeb, Rhoades and Co. has said that, "We will have more mergers because they are necessary...and conglomerate combinations will continue."

I. John Billera, president and chairman of U.S. Industries, Inc., has said that, for the next 10 to 15 years the service industries and consumer manufacturing firms will be the leaders in growth. He added that many companies may find that it will be better to turn attention to acquisitions than to face the long, expensive research needed to develop new products. "Acquisition is a form of research and development," said Billera, whose corporation is composed of 110 diversified companies.

The lesson to be learned from the conglomerates and one-bank holding companies is that creative minds in the corporate community will never stop seeking new and unusual solutions as long as mergers and acquisitions offer such a tempting way to enter the "go-go" parade.

Chapter 12

THE OVERSEAS MERGER MOVEMENT

The Outgrowth of Domestic Waves

A natural outgrowth of the accelerated merger and acquisition movement in the United States has been a significant rise in the number of overseas acquisitions by U.S. corporations. This latter development has followed in the wake of the spectacular rise during the post World War II years in U.S. private, direct investment abroad. Between 1950 and 1965, for example, U.S. business increased the value of its offshore investments by more than 400 percent!

The initial thrust of U.S. private investment abroad took the form of original investments–ventures in which the U.S. corporation "started from scratch," built plants, established marketing operations, and ran a wholly owned show. But local nationalism, fears of foreign (U.S.) domination, and resurgent industrial growth began to change the pattern. Soon U.S. firms found it attractive to merge with established foreign concerns, to exchange technical know-how and capital for established production and marketing organizations. Conditions were ripe for the birth of a world-wide merger and acquisition movement and U.S. corporations were eager midwives.

Spurring the movement along in recent years has been the gradual acceptance of *truly* international business, which means the organization of production in the context of international rather than national resource allocation, and the development of marketing concepts that meet the needs and demands of a global market place. This has resulted in the creation of a new kind of international business enterprise–truly international in its ownership, in its management, in its outlook, and in its approach to growth and expansion.

The Value of U.S. Investments Abroad

The growth of the total book value of U.S. foreign direct investments has been phenomenal, increasing eight fold in terms of "current dollars" in one generation. And it is still increasing at a spectacular rate. Aggregate U.S. direct investment abroad exceeded $60 billion by the end of 1969 and estimates indicate that U.S. corporations are not slackening the pace. Despite the U.S. government's mandatory controls on capital outflows, overseas investment outlays jumped some 22 percent or $13.2 billion in 1970 and are expected to increase by $15.3 billion in 1971 for still another record. Interestingly, American business produces goods abroad worth six times what it exports from the United States; at least $200 billion worth of products compared with exports valued at some $35 billion.

The big gains are marked for Canada and Western Europe, while companies indicate they will invest only a little more in Latin America and other less-developed areas. The reason, of course, is that investments are keyed to economic growth abroad and the resurgent West European economies have apparently inspired investors' confidence. This is in contrast to the situation in 1968, when a European slow down and over-capacity in Canada caused U.S. concerns to curb new investments in the traditionally favored areas.

The history of U.S. direct investments abroad reveals a pattern of change that reflects both foreign economic development and industrial preferences on the part of American investors. Initially, and into the early 1950s, Latin America received the largest single share of U.S. investment, and "yankee" dollars were concentrated in rails, mining, oil, and tropical agriculture. By 1967, however, Canada had taken the lead with an aggregate total of $18 billion, and manufacturing and petroleum investments accounted for almost three-fourths of the value of private capital outlays of just under $60 billion. Projections for 1971 showed a total of $2.8 billion earmarked for Canada and $2.4 billion for Latin America.

It was Europe, however, that captured America's fancy and company after company rushed to build manufacturing plants to take advantage of the Continent's post-war economic "miracle." American companies led the way in developing Europe-wide industries and marketing organizations to capitalize on the newly formed European Economic Community (France, West Germany, Italy, Belgium, the Netherlands, and Luxembourg). By the late 1960s the rush had temporarily slowed, but Europe with a total value of $17 billion was already running a close second to Canada as the area of greatest U.S. foreign direct investment. In the meantime, such previously neglected areas as the Far East, Oceania, Africa, and other Western Hemisphere countries had climbed to an aggregate of more than $11 billion, or slightly more than the Latin American total investment of $10 billion. Projections for 1971 pointed to increases of $4.0 billion for the Common Market, $2.5 billion for the rest of Europe, $0.8 billion for Oceania, and $2.8 billion for all others.

Europe's Merger Tide

In Europe, corporate size has never created the concern it does in the United States. In fact, in recent years European corporations have been encouraged to join forces to present a more formidable barrier to American takeover. Moreover, the Treaty of Rome, which brought the European Economic Community (EEC) into being, says nothing about size per se in its articles on antitrust. Instead, in obvious deference to the heyday of the pre-1945 corporate giant, it cautions for the most part only against actual restraint of competition. The gospel of bigness is as sacred as ever.

Despite an open invitation to merger and acquisition, however, European companies have tended to keep their consolidation moves within their own national borders. With some notable exceptions, there has been very little border crossing by merging corporations. One reason for this is the failure thus far by the EEC to harmonize corporate and tax laws.

Some Success Stories

Yet, multinational consolidations are taking place, often involving an American partner. One suitable approach is the one recently utilized by Algemene Kunstzijde Unie (AKU) N.V. of the Netherlands and Union Chimique-Chemische Bedrijven (UCB) S.A. of Belgium. They "Europeanized" their operations by having AKU take over UCB's synthetic fiber production division in Belgium in exchange for transferring to UCB two paper and plastics plants in the Netherlands, in addition to 650,000 ordinary AKU shares.

AKU, a corporation with extensive foreign interests, early in 1969 acquired most of the stock of Satig AG of Glarus, Switzerland, following a year of close cooperation between the Dutch firm and a Sastig subsidiary in Switzerland, Feldmuehle AG.

Typical of European mergers designed to enable the combined corporation to better compete in world markets was the agreement between two leading electrical companies—Allmaenna Svenska Elektriska AB(ASEA) of Sweden and Brown, Boveri & Cie AG (BBC) of Switzerland—to cooperate in certain operational areas, while continuing to compete in others. This includes a licensing contract enabling Stal-Laval Turbin AB, an ASEA subsidiary, to use BBC steam turbine techniques.

In the works is a merger of West Germany's two largest aircraft makers—Messerschmitt-Boelkow, itself the result of a 1967 merger, and Hamburg Flugzevgbua. Messerschmitt has two foreign share holders, the Boeing Company of Seattle and Nord Aviation of Paris. Each holds 16.66 percent.

With this merger, urged by the German government, the only other German aircraft makers will be Vereinigte Flugtechnische Werke (VFW) of Bremen, and Dornier

Aircraft Makers of Friedrichshafen. Krupp is the largest shareholder in VFW, but United Aircraft Corporation of Hartford, Conn. holds 26.4 percent.

The Case of Westinghouse

One of the most significant acquisition attempts in Europe by an American company was the long simmering bid by Westinghouse Electric Corporation to take over controlling interest in Jeumont-Schneider, a none-too-successful French company.

The Westinghouse plan, blocked by French President Georges Pompidou, called for Jeumont-Schneider to become the base of a giant, Europe-wide complex for manufacturing heavy electrical equipment. The arms of the complex would be formed when Westinghouse took over and merged its licensees in Belgium, Italy, and Spain.

Westinghouse hoped that Pompidou, like President Charles de Gaulle before him, would have a change of heart. Some years ago DeGaulle blocked General Electric's bid to buy Machines Bull, France's then-troubled computer manufacturer. DeGaulle later yielded when the "French Solution" he was backing proved unworkable.

Observers feel Westinghouse may now take another route. The U.S. company may go ahead with plans to merge some of its European licensees—probably Belgium's ACEC, Italy's Ercole Marelli and Franco Tosi, and Spain's Anemessa—to create a company substantial enough to compete with Britain's English Electric and Germany's AEG and Siemens. The new group, most likely headquartered in Brussels, could then attempt to work out a production agreement with Jeumont-Schneider.

Meanwhile, the French President is expected to urge Baron Edouard-Hean Empain, who owns 61 percent of Jeumont-Schneider, as well as 30 percent of ACEC, Westinghouse's Belgian licensee, to sell the French company to CGE-Alsthom, France's biggest electrical group. The resulting French giant could then work with Germany's Siemens and AEG to develop a nuclear energy entente that is being pushed in Bonn and Paris. Such are the international corporate machinations that promise to draw U.S. companies ever deeper into the flood tide of European mergers.

Foreign Antitrust Considerations

Generally speaking, of all the industrialized nations, the United States has the most rigid rules and regulations governing mergers and acquisitions (see also Chapter 8.) As mentioned earlier, bigness itself is not regarded as an evil abroad, nor is the "possibility" that competition "may be" restricted. Most foreign antitrust laws concern themselves with whether restraint of trade and competition actually exist. The corporate giants of pre-World War II Germany and Japan were indications of this long-accepted concept.

Now, some 25 years after the break up of the German and Japanese combines, the giants are returning on the scene. One reason is the demand of the global market place; another is the stated intention to block the American takeover of key national industries.

Typical of current overseas thinking is Japan's reevaluation of its prewar holding company system. A study group of the Federation of Economic Organizations (Keidaren) is drafting a plan that would resurrect this powerful industrial gambit. If accepted, the move would result in a revision of Japan's anti-monopoly law.

Behind Keidaren's move is the feeling that Japan's financial and industrial position is vulnerable to foreign takeover attempts, and that it is becoming more so as trade and investment liberalization continues.

Keidaren, Japan's most powerful business organization, advocates changing the anti-monopoly law to permit the big companies to maintain controlling interest in minor firms and to form centralized combines. The plan would fit in nicely with the country's present tide of mergers and acquisitions.

There is no question that the Japanese business community, and the general public (like those in many European countries), are ready to accept the monopoly concept. In Japan, for example, there was a noticeable lack of a public uproar when Yawata Iron and Steel and Fuji Iron and Steel announced a merger in late 1969.

Foreign Joint Ventures and U.S. Business

Joint ventures have been a part of America's expanding industrial scene for a great many years, and the trend has spread abroad. In 1966, 218 joint ventures were reported by American corporations. The following year the number dropped to 171, but the pace has quickened ever since.

What is a joint venture: Is it a trial diversification move in lieu of an immediate merger or acquisition? Or is it a method of joining forces in a common effort without going the full merger route involving other products and endeavors which are not of interest to either party?

Observers of joint ventures see them as a diversification move. For example, steel companies are joining with other metals companies, particularly aluminum. And, this offers a measure of protection because of the inroads of competing metals into the fields held by steel in the past.

The simplest and narrowest definition of joint venture is the formation of a new company owned in common by two or more firms. Another view is that the joint venture comprises any form of association which implies collaboration for more than a transitory period. This definition stresses the human and psychological aspect, rather than the legal.

Getting the Edge in the International Market

Joint ventures attract American businessmen to join hands with other American corporations and with foreign corporations, government agencies, or entrepreneurs to develop new products, to share the high costs of exploration, to enter new markets, to build huge industrial complexes, and to exploit mining and real estate potentials around the globe.

On the international business scene, corporations of capital-exporting countries have come to realize that their foreign business interests can no longer be kept entirely in the hands of the investing businesses, as was common in England and Holland. The interests and desires of the host country must be taken into account. In the postwar period, the international joint venture has become an important transmission belt for relating the resources of industrially developed nations to the needs and aspirations of less developed countries. Thus, the international joint venture bridges the gap between the vast materials and technological superiority of the great industrial nations and the requirements of nations that are in the building process.

Some Cases In Point

Many foreign countries are leaders in the joint venture field. Japan, probably the greatest exponent of the joint venture, is followed by Italy, West Germany and Mexico. For example, Japan, long fearing U.S. efforts to restrict Japanese imports, recently agreed to relax their own restrictions on foreign investments, which had blocked U.S. automobile companies' efforts to move into the Japanese market. Under new agreements, foreign manufacturers will be permitted to establish joint ventures to assemble cars in Japan. This might also be considered a *quid pro quo,* since Japanese cars have moved strongly into the American market.

The great variety of joint ventures is shown by a few examples. International Paper, Inc., world's largest paper manufacturer, has been studying the establishment of a joint venture with Daishowa Paper Manufacturing Company of Tokyo to sell pulpwood to Japanese paper manufacturers. Kaiser Aluminum & Chemical Corporation and Placer Development, Ltd. of Canada plan to expand their exploration efforts and alumina development activities in Australia, Papua and New Guinea.

For a number of years Foster Wheeler Corporation has worked with John Brown Boilers Ltd. in Great Britain in the production of steam generators for public power, industrial applications and marine propulsion. The joint venture, originally 50-50, has become by mutual consent weighted in favor of Foster Wheeler. The joint corporation operated a huge manufacturing complex at Hartlepool, England.

Getting the Joint Venture Off the Ground

How do joint ventures get started? Usually, they spring from the possibility of joint gain, and are consummated by each company putting something into the joint venture. Globe Industries Inc. of Chicago, a manufacturer of a significant amount of the sound-deadening panels used in automobiles, had been supplying the O.E.M. market in Canada through exports. Recently, however, Globe established with Somerville Industries, Ltd. of Canada, a joint venture called Mastico Inc. Globe contributed its know-how and operating management to the project and Somerville contributed top management and its knowledge of how to manufacture and market in the Canadian market.

Once a joint venture is established, it has the same problem confronting any other corporation. There must be a business objective, a board of directors, and management. The product or products must be manufactured and marketed and financial records must be kept, as in any other corporation. Each partner puts up the necessary funds, although negotiations may establish the dollar contributions in other than equal amounts. One partner may contribute a manufacturing plant, another a marketing system, or know-how. Each contribution has a value which must be considered in the establishment of the joint venture.

Regulations Can Be Complex

Overseas joint ventures must take into account the great variety of statutory regulations. Some nations will not permit a foreign group or corporation to own control of a corporation within their boundaries. Many foreign joint ventures involving U.S. companies, therefore, find the American corporation owning a minority interest.

There are numerous restrictions governing the movement of profits out of the host country. Corporate executives when confronted with these regulations have to make a "go" or "no-go" decision. If they believe that as the venture prospers, earnings will be plowed back to make the joint venture expand and grow, then the decision may be positive. Furthermore, the financial officials of the American corporation must constantly review the monetary problems, perhaps setting up hedges against currency devaluations and planning through host company officials for repatriation of some of the profits as dividends to the American corporation. There are risks and uncertainties in foreign joint ventures, but as the world grows smaller and more interdependent, confidence is undoubtedly growing that foreign nations will see values in working with American corporations.

The trade-off can be a good one for any progressive, far seeing foreign government official. On the one hand, foreign capital is entering the country in partnership with local industry to accomplish what is not possible alone locally. It is a small enough sacrifice to permit some of the profits to leave the country, since the end result may be an even greater inflow of much-needed capital and technology.

The foregoing touches on some of the problems inherent in joint ventures. There may be disagreements on investments, earnings disposal, and on the direction and scope the joint venture will have. There are certain to be differences among the managements and boards of directors, largely because of the backgrounds of the various officers. However, this is all part of the developing, industrial "One World," and the individuals concerned have shown a remarkable ability over the past generation to cope with and conquer these problems.

Overcoming Communication Problems

On occasion, the expression "joint venture" is misused as is the term "merger." One American corporation, for example, purchased a 10 percent interest in a company in Spain. The company was small and it was not able to produce products which were being manufactured in the United States and sold in Spain through the efforts of the partner company. The management of the American corporation spoke of the arrangement as a joint venture, and said that it was in the business of some manufacturing and marketing. But from a legal standpoint, the U.S. concern merely had an investment in a foreign corporation, made possible by the movement of currency from the American corporation's English subsidiary. This raises another aspect of foreign joint ventures; while the foreign nation may limit repatriation of dividends to the United States, it is usually willing to permit the movement of money to other countries which have historically been in its currency bloc.

Joint ventures have their purposes, their problems and their profits. Otherwise, there would not be continued expansion in that field. They are probably less often used as the road to acquisition on foreign soil than in the United States, although their use abroad is growing rapidly.

As a method of bringing companies together for mutual advantage, they share the spotlight with mergers and acquisitions. If not a direct part of the latter movement, as explained in this book, they are certainly first cousins.

As the world grows smaller, they are certain to increase in number and importance. The progressive executive bent on expanding his company through new products and acquisition must look upon joint ventures as another fruitful and profitable avenue of expansion. This is particularly true with respect to the steadily growing expansion of U.S. business abroad.

APPENDIX

BUSINESS APPRAISAL CHECK LIST

Responsibility	*Responsible Officer*	*Status*	*Comment*
I. The Corporation			
1. Original Name and Purpose			
2. When Founded			
3. Changes in Corporate Name or Purpose			
4. Description of Present Business			
5. Ownership			
6. States in which Qualified to do Business			
7. Location of Facilities and Branches			
II. Management			
1. Organization Chart			
2. Number of Employees by Departments			
3. Directors and Officers			
4. Key Employees			
5. Employment Contracts			
Consultants and outside Services Utilized			

Responsibility	*Responsible Officer*	*Status*	*Comment*
6. Wage Employees			
a. Union contract status			
b. Present labor situation			
c. Job classifications and rates			
7. Personnel Policies and Practices			
a. Working rules			
b. Stock options			
c. Bonus arrangements			
d. Profit-sharing			
e. Pension plan			
III. Financial			
1. Balance Sheet			
2. Cash Position			
3. Projection of Cash Flow			
4. Receivables— condition, turnover, bad debt experience			
5. Inventories— Amount in raw material, work in process, and finished goods			
6. Working Capital Position			
7. Investments			
8. Employee Loans			
9. Prepaid Expenses			
10. Deferred Charges			

Responsibility	*Responsible Officer*	*Status*	*Comment*
11. Properties:			
a. Depreciation and rates			
b. Insurance coverage			
12. Liabilities			
a. Accounts payable			
b. Contingent liabilities			
13. Profit and Loss Statement			
14. Analysis of Manufacturing Costs and Gross Profits; Relative Proportions of Labor, Material, and Manufacturing Overhead			
15. Expenses:			
a. Selling			
b. Administrative and general			
16. Analysis of Profit from Operations			
17. Final Surplus Net Profit			
18. Earnings Record for 5-Year Period			
19. Dividend Record for 5-Year Period—Stock or Cash			
IV. Products			
1. Major Classifications and Relative Importance			
2. Competition			

Responsibility	*Responsible Officer*	*Status*	*Comment*
3. Brands or Trade Names			
4. Seasonal Sales Pattern			
5. Markets and Prices			
6. Government Business:			
a. Description of product			
b. Status of contracts—prime or sub-contract			
c. Status of facilities contracts			
d. Methods of pricing			
e. Future business outlook			
f. Status of renogiations			
g. Security status			
V. Sales			
1. Distribution—Types Used			
2. Geographical Distribution			
3. Lists and Ratings of Principal Customers			
4. Concentration of Sales Among Principal Accounts			
5. Sales Organization:			
a. Branch offices			
b. Compensation of salesmen			
c. Manufacturing representatives			

Responsibility	*Responsible Officer*	*Status*	*Comment*
6. Sales Policies:			
a. Pricing			
b. Discounts			
c. Service and returns			
d. Forecasting			
e. Market research			
7. Advertising and Promotion			
a. Internal activities			
b. Agency retained			
c. Current costs			
d. Budgets			
VI. Fixed Assets			
1. Land and Buildings			
2. Equipment			
3. Services and Utilities			
VII. Manufacturing			
1. Assembly Methods			
2. Quality Control and Inspection			
3. Salvage			
4. Material Handling			
5. Storage and Warehousing			
6. Safety			
7. Use of Computers			
VIII. Engineering and Research			
1. Facilities			
2. Research and Development			
3. Importance to product			

Responsibility	*Responsible Officer*	*Status*	*Comment*
IX. Miscellaneous			
1. List of Patents			
2. Patent Agreements with Employee			
3. "No Compete" Agreements with Employees on Leaving Company			
4. Applicable State Laws			
5. By-Laws			
6. Minute Books			
7. Stock Books			
8. Leases			
9. Contracts			
10. Debentures			
11. Loan Agreements with Banks and Insurance Companies			
X. Controls, Financial, Etc.			
1. Computerization of Payroll, Receivables Inventory etc.			

INDEX

INDEX

H

I

M

N

O

P